Trap Doors
and
Trojan Horses

TRAP DOORS
AND
TROJAN HORSES

An Auditing Action Adventure

D. Larry Crumbley

Lawrence Murphy Smith

Laura Davis DeLaune

CAROLINA ACADEMIC PRESS

Durham, North Carolina

HF
5667
·C73
2009

Library of Congress Cataloging-in-Publication Data

Crumbley, D. Larry.
Trap doors and trojan horses : an auditing action adventure / D.
Larry Crumbley, Lawrence Murphy Smith, Laura Davis DeLaune.
    p. cm.
ISBN 978-1-59460-696-0 (alk. paper)
1. Auditing. 2. Auditing--Fiction. I. Smith, Lawrence Murphy.
II. DeLaune, Laura Davis. III. Title.
HF5667.C73 2009
657'.45--dc22

                                    2009012056

Carolina Academic Press
700 Kent Street
Durham, North Carolina 27701
Telephone (919) 489-7486
Fax (919) 493-5668
www.cap-press.com

Printed in the United States of America

Auditing is a systematic process of objectively obtaining and evaluating evidence regarding assertions about economic actions and events to ascertain the degree of correspondence between the assertions and established criteria and communicating the results to interested users.

—Committee on Basic Accounting Concepts
American Accounting Association

Dedicated to
Cynthia Cooper

Contents

Preface

This supplementary novel may be used near the end of an auditing or beginning of a data processing or forensic accounting course. It would be ideal for an MBA program that has a light coverage of accounting. The novel could be used in CPA firms' in-house training programs. This educational novel illustrates the differences between a regular audit and the investigation required by forensic accountants to uncover computer fraud. Every business executive should read it, because just as termites never sleep, fraud never sleeps. Just like termites, fraud can destroy the foundation of an entity.

The novel mixes fraud, crime, politics, ethics, computer techniques, expert witnessing, and auditing for a better and easier way to learn accounting. If used as a supplement to an auditing, forensic accounting, fraud examination, or a computer course, this exciting novel provides a painless way of learning auditing principles. The suspenseful story combines computer and auditing concepts in a fashion even a novice can understand and enjoy. With computer fraud losses reaching $300 billion per year, accountants must be familiar with electronic auditing.

Professor Lenny Cramer operates a small forensic accounting firm in Atlanta, Georgia. As a forensic accountant, he goes beyond recordkeeping and looks at the records to learn and gather information. Called "a sort of Indiana Jones of the Ledger Set" by the Washington Post, Lenny teaches in the classroom, testifies before a Congressional committee, and serves as an expert witness in the courtroom. In *Trap Doors and Trojan Horses*, he and his sidekick, Slam Duncan, investigate a mysterious series of computer losses at a division of Coca-Cola. Coke, of course, is one of the world's most popular and best recognized consumer products.

Cramer and Duncan employ auditing and computer concepts in making real-life decisions. Along the way, business practices, ethics, political controversies, contemporary individual and corporate planning, accounting fraud, and the lives of CPAs and their colleagues are elucidated in a way both students and instructors will find gripping and informative. This instructive and entertaining approach is an excellent substitute for a mundane practice set. A novel shows accounting students that the accounting profession is much better than the stereotype image most people have. An effective accountant is bright, personable, skeptical, and technically competent. As geologist Charles Lyell said many years ago, "never call an accountant a credit to his profession; a good accountant is a debit to his profession."

The authors acknowledge the work on the beginning chapters by Hugh Nations. The authors are grateful to the following people for their review and comments on earlier versions of the novel: Teresa Conover, James C. Flagg, Steve Flory, David Kerr, R. Stephen McDuffie, Alfred R. Michenzi, Jeffrey R. Miller, Barbara Morris, Kibily D. Samake, Bittany Samrow, Valerie Scheffler, Winston T. Shearon, Katherine T. Smith, Robert Strawser, and James H. Thompson. Any shortcomings, however, remain the total responsibility of the authors.

D. Larry Crumbley
Baton Rouge, LA

L. Murphy Smith
College Station, TX

Laura Davis DeLaune
Baton Rouge, LA

By focusing on protagonists like the forensic accountant — the investigator of ledgers — a novel allows the otherwise dry accounting material to take on the aura of mystery. The dramatic intrigue, in turn, helps the reader retain the principles.

— *The Administrator*

* * *

Coca-Cola and Coke are registered trademarks. Most trademarks do not have definitely determinable useful lives, and the direct consideration paid for an intangible asset cannot be amortized.

* * *

The company accountant is shy and retiring. He's shy a quarter of a million dollars. That's why he's retiring.

— Milton Berle

Trap Doors
and
Trojan Horses

Chapter 1

Man is the only animal who drinks when he isn't thirsty.

—Mark Twain

Lenny Cramer could feel the grip of nagging tension relaxing its hold just the slightest as he drank his Cherry Coke. It brought back boyhood memories because the flavor was slightly reminiscent of the Cherry Cokes he used to drink at the soda fountain of his old neighborhood drugstore. He then thought about his new consulting job. He was rather pleased that the Coca-Cola Company had hired him. After all, Coke was a major international business firm. It was one of the 30 companies included in the Dow Jones Industrial Average, the stock market barometer. The thought of working for the company that manufactured this beverage made each sip particularly refreshing.

He and his daughter were now residing in Atlanta, the queen city of the South. As he thought about his new home, Cramer began recalling scenes from the epic motion picture, *Gone With The Wind*. He had a passion for history and had read numerous books about the Civil War. As wars go, it was an exceptionally tragic one. Families were divided by the conflict. Even President and Mrs. Lincoln had family members fighting on each side. The city of Atlanta was burned to the ground by the Union forces under General William Tecumseh Sherman. For many years, people with the surname of Sherman felt a little uncomfortable living in Georgia.

Cramer looked at his daughter and mused with a twinge of regret. Rebecca soon would be partaking of all the joys that adulthood holds—independence, self-reliance, marriage, children; not to mention, mortgages, ulcers, traffic jams, high gasoline prices, income taxes, and the daily grind. At 14, Rebecca was already beginning to show the promise of exuberant womanhood. Her nose was a trifle long, a legacy from the Cramer side of the family that immediately stamped them as father and daughter, but her wide-set eyes gave an air of constant crinkling delighted surprise that Cramer knew would one day devastate the young men who crossed her path. His late wife hadn't been beautiful, but he had counted himself lucky to win her over the many suitors who, like himself, had fallen into those same eyes and found themselves snared. Watching Rebecca as she had walked away to the ladies' room, Cramer had felt a warm envy for his daughter's next 10 or 12 years. Adolescence and college and just getting started in his profession had been some of the most exciting years of his life, he reflected. And he suspected Rebecca would fit right into the Southern ambiance, despite her initial reluctance at leaving Philadelphia.

Just now, Cramer himself was feeling a bit uncomfortable, and after a moment he finally was able to identify the source. It was the atmosphere in the lobby bar at the Westin Peachtree Plaza. Well ... not the atmosphere so much as the surroundings.

On his earlier visits to the Georgia capital, Cramer had stayed at the Hyatt Regency. The Westin Peachtree Plaza was much newer than the Regency, and the lobby bar was one of the city's showcases. The tables were virtually islands set in an indoor lagoon, and being surrounded by so much water was having its effect. Cramer felt an unmistakable urge to visit the men's room, though he knew it wasn't really necessary. The professor smiled as he reflected that the same urge had probably been what nudged Rebecca to the ladies' room.

The Westin Peachtree Plaza was an extravagant edifice and the view from the Sun Dial, the revolving bar atop the 73-story hotel, was without parallel in the city. Rebecca and he had visited the revolving Sun Dial restaurant briefly last night, just long enough for each to have a soft drink. Cramer had been even uneasier then, and it had nothing to do with his kidneys. He just didn't like being stuck that high up with no way to get down in the event of a fire.

Cramer had to admit, however, that the view from the bar was worth the visit. Patrons could follow the course of world-famed Peachtree Street as it wound northward for miles through the city toward the affluent Sandy Springs and Roswell area. Looking out on the panorama, he had even been able to point out the imposing granite bulk of Stone Mountain to the east.

Just as the Westin Peachtree Plaza was an architectural extravagance, Cramer thought this stay was an extravagance for him as well with its floor-to-ceiling glass windows. On earlier visits, he had chosen more modest accommodations, but this time Rebecca was along for her introduction to her new home, and Cramer wanted to make it special for her. God knows she's been through enough in the past year, he recollected, even if he did try to shield her from as much as possible. Still, he knew there had been incidents. Rebecca's classmates had said some things after his trouble at the Wharton Business School at the University of Pennsylvania. She'd borne it well, but Cramer knew his sensitive daughter well enough to know that his troubles had left their marks. The move to Atlanta should prove a Godsend, Cramer mused, even if Rebecca wasn't crazy about the idea initially. The change would be a little rough at the beginning starting all over again in a new city. "If I could get through the past stressful year, though, I should be able to do just about anything," he thought.

Cramer randomly thought about how his elementary teacher used to call his musing 'wool gathering.' She'd always ask, "Are you planning to knit an afghan when you're through?" Rebecca's throaty voice pulled Cramer back from his reverie. He smiled inwardly: More than once, women of his acquaintance who had not met Rebecca had greeted him frostily after Rebecca answered the phone. Only after they learned that the voice was his adolescent daughter had their tone thawed. What a marvel, that voice, coming as it did from a youngster who couldn't decide yet which was more exciting, tennis or boys. Quickly, Cramer put away any thoughts of women. That did nothing but evoke thoughts of the last time he had seen Dana, his close friend clad in prison gray, her face drawn but still defiantly beautiful.

"Just thinking about all we have to do this week, Honey," Cramer replied. "We've got to move in when the van comes tomorrow, and then we must get the house in order. Of course, I must do the same with the office. We're going to be pretty busy for a few days, so I guess we'd better enjoy ourselves tonight. I forgot to tell you, Will and Emma want us to come over for dinner Friday night."

"I'd like that," Rebecca said. "How long has it been since I've seen them? Years and years. I remember the last time. They gave me Artemis. You're not going to tell them what happened to him, are you?"

Artemis was a stuffed lamb that the Poseys had given Becc. A smile flickered briefly across Cramer's face as he remembered how his wife, who hated nicknames, couldn't stop their daughter from attaining the nickname "Becc" after her friends adopted it. Their last visit to Philadelphia had, indeed, been years ago, and it had been a grand reunion of two old friends. It seemed they'd relived almost every one of their moments at Harvard, where both had earned MBAs. Cramer had been on the top of the heap at the time of that visit: a Distinguished Professor at Wharton, almost a sure shot for an accounting chair at the next vacancy, and a lucrative consulting business in auditing on the side.

Then the long nightmare had begun. For a time, it appeared that he would lose his Certified Public Accountant (CPA) certificate, and would face the ultimate humiliation of being reported in the semi-monthly *The CPA Letter* that he had been expelled from the accounting profession that he loved, but the plagiarizing charge that had begun his long fall into desolation had been proved false. If he had ever doubted it, Cramer at least had the satisfaction of knowing now that he practiced in a profession where ethics meant something.

The codes of the American Institute of CPAs (AICPA) and of the various state societies had teeth. However, even if he had been expelled or suspended from both the Pennsylvania Society of CPAs and the AICPA, he could still have practiced accounting — if he were able to find clients. Both organizations were voluntary societies. Only if the Pennsylvania Board of Accountancy had suspended or revoked his CPA certificate, which was effectively his union card, would he have lost his right to practice accounting.

But that hadn't happened. That numbing episode was all behind him now, and his old friend, Will Posey, had come to his rescue after Cramer's troubles had cost him his position and his

his library and electronic gear. The CPA had prided himself on having the best and latest in technology in Philadelphia, and he fully intended to adhere to that philosophy in Atlanta.

By the time Friday afternoon arrived, the house was sparkling and had begun to feel like a home, and the office was ready, expectantly waiting his arrival Monday morning. He and Rebecca knocked off, ready for the dinner with the Poseys and the weekend of visiting the Atlanta attractions that Cramer had promised.

Cramer even had time to browse through the latest copy of *The Quantum PC Report for CPAs.* One article in particular caught his eye. The author contended that eventually every hard drive on a computer will fail, with the resultant loss of all the programs and data on it. His solution was both obvious and simple: Make a copy, on a regular basis, of all the information on the drive.

The world surely would be better off if we'd all try the obvious, simple solutions to problems more frequently, Cramer thought just before easing off into a short but well-deserved nap.

* * *

"Got the office all ship-shape? Ready to hit the ground running Monday?" Will Posey asked Cramer. The two old friends were relaxing in the den as his wife and Becc were cleaning up after a home cooked meal. The dinner had almost made Cramer wince at the memories of what he had lost when his wife died. As a cook she had been the equal of Emma Posey.

"Well, I'm ready to hit the ground running, but I suspect it'll be at more of a trot," Cramer replied. "When a fellow reaches my age, the only time he runs is when something's chasing him."

"I know I've said this before, Will," Cramer continued, "but I do want you to know I appreciate everything you've done. If you hadn't been so insistent, I probably would have gone on moldering and moping in Philadelphia forever. I know you've gone out on a limb, and I'm grateful."

"Hey, I haven't done anything except to recommend that we hire the best CPA I know to do a little snooping for my division. You're a natural—one of the best experts around on forensic accounting and high technology."

"Well, I thought I fulfilled the first standard of the Generally Accepted Auditing Standards—competence. But after getting hoodwinked by Dana Scott, I sometimes wonder even about that," Cramer said wryly. "Prison gray is definitely not flattering on Dana." Posey brushed off his friend's protestations. "Love can blind anybody's judgment. How could you know that she would try to rip-off those diamonds and jewels in Rangoon? Now they call it Yangon. Besides, even CPAs have their professional escape hatches. Like they taught us, an ordinary audit is not primarily intended to detect fraud...."

"Unless the effect on the financial statements is material," Cramer interrupted. "At least I've got that down pat."

"Anyway, all it took was to bring the boss over one night and feed him one of Emma's pot roasts, and he was sold. Of course, I did have to hook a couple of shots at the club before we got home for dinner, but it was worth it to know you'll be getting off to a good start here. How do you like your new secretary? What's her name?"

"Michele Poe, and she seems great. She just got tired of that 30-mile round trip into town every day, even if she had to take a pay cut to avoid the traffic jams. Traffic must really be a hassle here in Atlanta, if she's willing to give up a good job with KPMG to come with me. She knows it will be quite a while before she'll be getting the salary and benefits she had with KPMG."

"Once you have the dubious opportunity to drive in Atlanta's five o'clock traffic, you'll understand why she feels that way. The only thing I can think of that's worse is being stuck in Phillips Arena when one of those heavy metal groups is tearing the place up. Makes me just about as nervous as being tied up on the Northeast Expressway. E&Y are our auditors. Who are the big CPA firms now?"

"In term of revenue, PricewaterhouseCoopers is first, Deloitte second, E &Y third, and KPMG fourth. Those mergers in the late eighties shook-up the pack. Losing Arthur Andersen because of their numerous fraudulent clients did not help."

Posey frowned, "Let me fill you in, though, on what to expect at the office when you start giving us the famous Cramer Crunch. As you know, we're not expecting a full-scale financial statement audit.

E&Y handles that, and does a fine job. After Sarbanes-Oxley, E&Y issues a report stating its opinion on the effectiveness of the internal controls over our financial reporting. Also, they issue a report on the fair presentation of Coke's financial statements in conformity with GAAP. Of course, you know that. But the boss thinks we need somebody to come in to make sure nothing really serious is going on. Here is a set of last year's financials."

"So what we're talking about is a forensic or operational audit," Cramer said, as he took the manila folder. "A systematic, detailed review of the activities of a narrow part of the business. My specified objective is to do an organized search for ways of improving efficiency and effectiveness. An OA focuses on information systems and operating procedures, and not on the actual dollar amounts or financial reporting information. Forensic auditing tends to look for fraud."

"OK, we'll call it a forensic audit, but do not look for dead people." Posey smiled. "Normally, all my division handles is the identification and initial development of overseas markets. It's up to us to keep up with what's going on around the globe, with an eye toward what will make a buck or two for Coke. Once a specified number of citizens of an underdeveloped nation reach a given income level, for example, it's up to my folks to know about it, and try to take advantage of it by opening up the market for Coke. It's a little more complicated than that, however. We have to factor in population concentration, for example, and the number of urban centers, and cultural influences. Basically, what it boils down to, though, is a numbers game. Oh, we also have to make sure that we haven't ticked off any banana republic prima donnas, or if we have, we have to sweet-talk them if it looks like maybe we want to set up a bottling plant on their front lawn."

Posey paused. "I'm asking you to constructively criticize our accounting procedures and controls." Posey lowered his voice, "What's happened is that something has come up that could be an embarrassment to the division—or at least to our divisional chief—in more ways than one."

Posey frowned and continued. "Joe's a good executive. I've never worked for anyone better. But he does have a problem maintaining high personal integrity. A little while back, he got involved with one of the women in the office. Apparently it all started with some 'innocent' flirting that unfortunately led to something more serious. Apparently, he does not follow Ronnie Milsap's country song, 'I'm a stand by my Woman Man.' What made it even more stupid for Joe is that her husband works for the division, too. One day, she's really bent out of shape with her husband. He'd promised her a new car and bought a bass boat instead, and she tells Joe that the guy is using the computer to play songs it's not supposed to play."

"Exactly what, she wouldn't or couldn't say, but she did know he'd paid cash for that boat. The lady cashes her husband's paycheck, so she knew he shouldn't have that kind of money. The problem is, Joe can't confront the thing directly. The lady and her husband are back on great terms again close as two Irishmen with only one beer between 'em."

"So you suspect fraud," Cramer suggested. "We are talking about a fraud or forensic audit. I like forensic audit better. It is more neutral. People hide and shut up when they hear the words fraud audit or fraud examination."

Posey nodded. "I agree to be careful about using the word fraud. Furthermore, there's another problem. Joe's on a fast track at the company, and he can't afford any kind of problems in his division that cause problems for other divisions. Our main computer system handles the billings to all of our bottlers, along with several miscellaneous operations. Some of the canned juice billings, for example, are on the system, and have been for about two years. And it handles many of the accounts payable for several divisions. That's temporary. Ultimately, these accounts payable are to be switched over to another part of the company, but the Syrup Set — that's what we call the other division that handles the syrup accounts — has got 'em for now."

"Who does the billings for the bottlers themselves?" Cramer asked. "Are those all franchises, or are some of them company-owned, and if they are, do they do their billing locally?"

"Hmmmmm … I forgot you're not an Atlantan," Posey smiled. "The Coca-Cola Company does very little bottling. Let me give you some history."

"The first Coke bottler was Joseph Biedenharn, a soda fountain operator in Vicksburg, Mississippi. That was in 1894. Then in 1897, two lawyers in Chattanooga, Tennessee, persuaded Coca-Cola President Asa Candler to give them the rights to bottle and sell Coca-Cola throughout the United States, except for Mississippi, Texas, and five New England states. The lawyers were Benjamin Franklin Thomas and Joseph Brown Whitehead. They were the real beginning of the franchise system that dominated Coke for almost a century, and they got a bargain. They paid only one dollar for the bottling rights."

"That was the bargain of the century," Cramer commented.

"Yeah. They paid less than the cost of a two-liter bottle of Coke today. Coke's got one of the most interesting corporate histories around. In the beginning an Atlanta pharmacist, John S. Pemberton, registered a trademark for 'French Wine Cola—ideal nerve and tonic stimulant.' His first advertisement appeared in the Atlanta Constitution in May 1886—'Delicious and Refreshing.' The concoction was wine with—get this—cocaine. The next year Pemberton deleted the wine and added caffeine and a kola nut extract. He changed the name to Coca-Cola, peddled it as 'brain food,' and sold it for 5¢ a glass. I remember one 1892 ad. It described Coke as 'The great brain and nerve tonic. Makes a pleasant and refreshing drink and is certain relief for some forms of headache.'"

"There are a lot of teenagers, including my own, who'll be glad to hear it's a brain tonic," Cramer chuckled.

"There's more," Posey continued. "Asa Candler was another guy who got a bargain with Coca-Cola. He was an Atlanta businessman, and in 1891 he bought all the rights to Coke from Pemberton for $2,300. Candler began selling the syrup to wholesalers, who sold it to drugstores to be mixed with carbonated water and sold at soda fountains. In 1919, the company was sold for $25 million. That's a return of about 10,870 percent in 28 years. I calculated it once. That comes out to a return of 388 percent per year. But as to the original point, Coca-Cola recently has been buying up its bottlers through a separate subsidiary called Coca-Cola Enterprises. Coke owns 49 percent of that operation. We're trying to consolidate. In 1950 there were more than a thousand bottlers. By 1985, they'd been reduced to 400, and we plan to continue to consolidate."

"When was Pepsi invented?"

"You cannot mention that word around anyone. Pepsi was invented in 1893, only a few years after Coke, by Caleb Bradham. He first called the drink 'Brad's Drink,' and he marketed it as a digestive aid and energy booster. Eventually it was renamed Pepsi-Cola because of its pepsin and kola nut contents."

Posey shifted on the light blue couch and spoke again. "But let's get back to our immediate problem. What Joe is worried about most is Jemima II." That's Jeremiah Mortimer Clifford II, who heads up the syrup crew. He and Joe go way back, which is where Jemima would like to send Joe. They're old college classmates, and there hasn't been a good feeling between them since Joe put a dead snake in Jemima's bed one night, and he actually wet his pants in front of half the Dartmouth lacrosse team. Joe's quite a one for pranks. Unfortunately, Jemima's even bigger on grudges than Joe is on pranks. He'd love to nail Joe's hide to the office door of the vice president for operations."

"That's why, *if* there's any hanky-panky going on with the computers, Joe's got to get a fix on it first. That way he not only can head off Jemima, but he can actually come out looking good … like he's on top of things."

"I'll do my best," Cramer promised.

"That's always been good enough for me," Will replied. "C'mon, let's go bore the girls with more of the old college days. And for goodness sake, don't mention that episode with Cathy Olfers when we were first-year graduate students. She and her husband live in Atlanta now, and I don't want to give Emma the idea that the flame's still burning."

Chapter 2

The audit of internal control should be integrated with the audit of the financial statements, so the auditor must plan and perform the work to achieve the objectives of both audits. This direction applies to all aspects of the audit, and it is particularly relevant to tests of controls.

— Public Company Accounting
Oversight Board (PCAOB),
October 17, 2007

Cramer was in the office by 7:30 a.m. Monday, and he already had a pot of coffee made and was on his second cup when his new secretary arrived. Michele Poe was an attractive woman, no doubt about it, but Cramer was not one of those executives who wanted just a pretty face at the front desk. He wanted competence, loyalty, and confidence, and he had gotten exactly that when he hired Michele. Judging by her recommendations, Michele's former employers were aware she wanted to find something closer to home, and had willingly but with obvious regret given her the highest recommendations. Furthermore, she suffused the whole office with the cheeriness of a field of daisies.

"It's going to be pretty slow around here for the first couple of days," Cramer said as he was packing his briefcase, "so if you've got any personal correspondence to catch up on, now's the time. About all that we need to do right now is to finish putting up the books and do whatever straightening up I didn't finish last week."

"This job may be the easiest I ever had," Michele said with a perky smile.

"Well, there is one other thing that should occupy you for a little while," Cramer noted. "Please look over my working papers." The accountant pointed to a stack of documents at least several inches high.

Michele looked at the stack. "This will take a while," she said with a grin. Glancing at the PC on her desk, Michele commented, "This PC looks up-to-date."

"You probably had something a bit more powerful at KPMG," Cramer said. "This PC will do everything we're going to need to do for a long time to come, though. Tell you what, plan to spend your time getting to be the most proficient operator in Atlanta on this setup. Then, when things start picking up, we'll be off to a running start. If you need me, I'll be at this number. Just ask for Will Posey, and he can track me down."

* * *

Based on the map, the trip to the Coca-Cola headquarters in downtown Atlanta from suburban Sandy Springs was a fairly direct one, using Roswell Road. Direct it was; quick it wasn't. Cramer got his first taste of the storied Atlanta traffic, a taste that threw him a quarter of an hour late. He noticed that Georgia Tech University was across the street from Coke. He didn't like being late, because Lenny Cramer was always on time, and his usually equable temperament was somewhat frayed when he finally arrived at Posey's office.

The Coke executive was an old friend of Cramer, but that didn't make Lenny feel any better about being late. As a veteran of years in the Atlanta traffic trenches, Posey was understanding and a trifle amused at his friend's discomfort. He quickly restored Cramer's equanimity and took Cramer to an available office where they discussed the audit.

Since this project was a forensic audit, there was no need for the CPA to follow many of the time-consuming steps a full audit would require. In a regular audit an accountant tests samples of inventory, receivables, and payables. The accountant will ask banks to confirm the amount of cash in the business's accounts and send form letters to outside companies that have contracts with the firm being audited. The purpose is to confirm that the other companies exist and that the various contracts or receivables are real.

Cramer was a forensic accountant. He specialized in uncovering fraud in ledgers of big and small companies. Aside from his CPA, Cramer had the following certificates: CrFA (Certified Forensic Accountant), CFFA (Certified Financial Forensic Analyst), and a CFF (Certified in Financial Forensics). The CFF was a recent designation of the AICPA, and he had just received his CFF. Cramer liked to quote from a piece in the *Wall Street Journal*: "Other accountants may look at the charts. But forensic accountants actually dig into the body." The increase in malpractice suits against the big accounting firms and the huge fraud cases in the early 2000s—such as Enron, WorldCom, and HealthSouth—had created a need for accountants specializing in detecting fraud.

One old example which Cramer used in his auditing class was the notorious Equity Funding fraud. Here nonexistent insurance policy records were added to the customers master file of the organization. This fiction was created by unscheduled file updating outside the mainstream of normal data processing operations. In Equity Funding the fraudsters colluded for nine years. Then there was the example of Penn Central Railroad "misplacing" almost 400 railroad cars. The computerized system was modified so that the missing rail cars would not be noticed.

A more recent 2008 brazen fraud was 70-year-old Bernie Madoff's $50 billion Ponzi scheme. Madoff was the investment manager of the Ascot Partners hedge fund which was offering double-digit returns to investors. The investment vehicle, Sterling Equities, which owns the New York Mets baseball team, had $300 million invested with Madoff. The Ponzi scheme was paying double-digit returns to some older investors with new investment funds. Although the SEC had been tipped as early as 1999 that Madoff was running a Ponzi scheme, their examiners found nothing on several tries. The SEC's budget is approximately $500 million.

Accountants and investors must be skeptical. Trust, but verify was Cramer's motto. If something is too good to be true, there is probably fraud involved.

In fact, even as a forensic audit the task promised to be a relatively abbreviated engagement. Coke's divisional chief suspected one of his staff of improper practices. Thus, Cramer could confine his review, at least initially, to the activities of the suspect. He might have to give the appearance of a broader audit, just to avoid tipping off any inquisitive and particularly observant employees, but the inquiry would still target just one individual.

But Cramer agreed with the Public Company Accounting Oversight Board (PCAOB) and its position that an "auditor's evaluation of entity-level controls can result in increasing or decreasing the testing that the auditor otherwise might have performed on other controls. If the auditor designs an audit approach with an expectation that certain entity-level controls (e.g., controls in the control environment) will be effective and those controls are not effective, the auditor might re-evaluate the planned audit approach and decide to expand his or her audit procedures." Auditors could not ignore the PCAOB.

The era of self-regulation by the accounting profession ended on April 16, 2003, when the PCAOB began setting auditing, attestation, quality control, and ethical standards for public auditing companies. The Sarbanes-Oxley Act changed the auditing profession's self-regulatory environment under the American Institute of Certified Public Accountants'(AICPA) peer review system to the regulatory framework under the PCAOB and the SEC oversight function for public accounting firms that audit financial statements of public companies.

The suspect was Dan Mays. From all outward appearances, Mays was an unlikely candidate to be playing games with Coca-Cola's corporate checkbook. He had been with this division for 12 of the 19 years he had been with Coke, beginning as a computer operator. But Cramer knew that many fraudsters were "trusted employees." After attending night school and taking a junior college associate degree in business, Mays had worked himself up to the point where he was in charge of payroll for the international division.

Cramer began his limited walkthrough by first conferring with the supervisor of overseas development. An auditor should perform "walkthroughs" of a business' significant processes. The PCAOB suggests that an auditor should "confirm his or her understanding by performing procedures that include making inquiries of and observing the personnel that actually perform the controls; reviewing documents that are used in, and that result from, the application of the controls; and comparing supporting documents (for example, sales invoices, contracts, and bills of lading) to the accounting records."

The supervisor explained that his division was looking at its computer requirements, and Cramer asked for a brief outline of the operations the supervisor needed the computer to do. He got more than he requested. For 45 minutes, he listened to a long and exquisitely detailed explanation of the needs for the overseas development crew, and a string of complaints. Cramer finally managed to rid himself of the overzealous executive, but not before he had been promised "a full, complete draft of our ongoing and vastly expanded needs within 48 hours." The CPA pledged to review the draft carefully, and gratefully ushered the visitor out the door.

The next two interviews went more swiftly, and by 11:30 Cramer was ready to talk to the payroll chief, who all along had been the only one he was really interested in. The other interviews had only been smoke screens that Cramer hoped would allay any suspicions the target of the audit might have. He wanted to get a first-hand look at Mays. Face-to-face conferences were not a required auditing tool, but Cramer had more than once learned that taking personal measure of an adversary could be productive. Cramer knew that one needed to have some first hand observations of a person before an interviewer could spot someone lying. He wished he had a second person to help in the interview to listen and act as a witness.

"I guess Joe explained that we're taking a look at the division's computer requirements," Cramer said as he ushered Mays into his small office. "This discussion is just a quick run-through for me, to give me some on-the-ground grasp of what you're doing now, and what the divisional personnel think we should be doing, if anything. Obviously, we'll be going into a lot more depth later, and you'll be talking with other consultants in a lot more detail. I'm just a CPA with limited computer expertise, but we want to be sure what procedures you have in place so we'll know what changes are indicated, if any. How about giving me a quick run-down on how you handle your end of things."

Mays quickly launched into an explanation of the payroll process. The discussion was all general, Cramer noted, except that Mays did seem to dwell a trifle long on the accounting safeguards included in payroll production. On the other hand, the CPA reflected, perhaps I'm just being overly suspicious. Cramer wanted to maintain control by clearly establishing the facts and to counter future denials.

"Do you just handle payroll," Cramer finally asked, "or do you have other functions?"

"Well," Mays responded, "we have some accounts payable … minor stuff, like office supplies and such. I take care of those, but they're pretty small. Just stuff central purchasing doesn't normally carry. Maybe flowers when one of the employees has a loss in the family, and that sort of thing. We pay all of those on the basis of vouchers that both Joe and I have to sign."

Cramer knew that body language was important in any interview or interrogation. An innocent person will sit upright in the chair, maintain strong eye contact, and give quick answers and denials. They may become angry or hostile. Whereas a guilty person may be more passive, playing a cat and mouse game with false clues. Untruthful answers may cause dry mouth and lips that result in a clicking sound when speaking. A dishonest person may avoid eye contact or stare at the interviewer and then drop the eyes down or away as they answer a question. Restlessness and shifting in a chair, abnormal eye-blink rate, and biting of the lips or tongue are other tell-tale signs of dishonest answers. An auditor has to observe both verbal and nonverbal signals during the investigative process.

Cramer wrapped up the interview just before lunch, as he had planned. He'd wanted to listen to and take a measure of Mays, not answer any questions. Thus, the timing of the interview was part of Cramer's plan. Lunchtime gave Cramer the excuse to cut off discussion when he'd sized up the payroll clerk.

The CPA had made previous arrangements to meet Posey at the Renaissance in downtown Atlanta. It was unlikely that anybody else from the division would be frequenting that restaurant, Posey had explained, and lunch would give the two time to review the morning's events.

"Looks like you're becoming a veteran of Atlanta traffic already," Posey grinned, sliding a Coke toward Cramer as he eased into a chair. "You're only seven minutes late."

"I am reminded of the injunction, 'All things come to him who waits,'" Cramer sighed. "I hope so, because it seems I'll be spending a large part of my life from now on waiting in mini-traffic jams."

"Don't worry about it. You may be late but you're impeccably dressed."

Cramer laughed. "What can I say, Will? The auditor's dress code in the old days was a dark, preferably pin-striped, suit. Let's face it, clients trust conservatively dressed auditors. Besides, I've noticed you business executives 'dress for success' the same way." Cramer paused to smile. "At least I *look* like I know what I'm doing." Both men grinned at Cramer's self-deprecation.

"How's it going in the office?" Posey queried. "Found any skunks in any woodpiles?"

"I haven't even begun looking for a woodpile yet," Cramer said. "I've talked to your man Mays, though, along with a couple of other chaps. He seems cool enough. Certainly is ready to convince you at the drop of a double-entry ledger that the payroll system is close to foolproof. And that's without even being asked."

"So what's next on the agenda?"

"Well, I've got one more interview set up for this afternoon. It isn't necessary, but I don't want to spook Mays. This way, I'm hoping he won't get the idea that I'm focusing on him. After that comes an examination of the payroll records, starting with Mays himself. If we're lucky, and if there is something going on, we'll find it right off. If not, then we'll expand the scope of things."

"Good. I told you about Jeanne Saxet. She's been with Joe ever since he joined Coca-Cola. I'd stake my reputation, such as it is, on her discretion, and so would Joe. In fact, considering his occasional philandering, he probably has. Joe has assigned Jeanne to you for whatever time you need her. She knows just about anything you should need to know about office routine, recordkeeping, and the whole nine yards. Plus she is thoroughly versed on our computer operation."

"Good," Cramer replied, just as the prime rib arrived. "I'll need her this afternoon, as soon as I finish with this final interview. That's when we'll start actually trying to determine what Mr. Mays has been up to. If anything."

* * *

Cramer had three possible ways to audit the computer records without calling in a bunch of IT auditors like many of the large CPA firms would do. First, he could use the vouching approach to audit around the computer. Using the oldest form, he could treat the computer as a "black box" and avoid any scrutiny of the computer system itself. He could follow the audit trail up to where computer processing began and then pick up the trail on the other side of processing by examining printouts. However, auditing standards specify that an auditor must develop a knowledge of the computer and may not rely on computer specialists. Computer systems now often generate a huge quantity of data which are beyond the scope of ticking and checking the transaction documents. Auditing around the computer is acceptable only where certain conditions are met. Specifically, this approach is appropriate where justified on a cost/benefit basis as compared to other available techniques. This approach is never appropriate where its use is solely justified by the auditor's lack of IT expertise.

Under the second approach — the verification method — an auditor develops independent means of verifying the existence, ownership, and valuation of assets. For example, in a regular audit, Cramer would use an inquiry program to obtain a sample printout of the computerized account files and then confirm these balances by circularizing the account holders.

Under the third option, the systems approach, the auditor appraises the control features of the computer system to determine if the objectives of the system have been met. If the computer controls are effective, then the auditor can generally assume that the data output is correct, assuming that the input data is correct.

Cramer decided to use the verification approach. He began by immediately zeroing in on the suspect, pulling up on the computer all of Mays' pay records for the past two years and comparing them with the actual paperwork. The CPA was looking for differences between computer entries and the paper trail left by the division's accounting system. If Mays was as astute as he had appeared in the interview, Cramer knew the rifle-shot approach would be a long shot, but it was worth a try. And, as things turned out, that's all it ended up being—just a try. The computer entries tallied perfectly with the accompanying paperwork.

Cramer had been looking for one dodge in particular. This scam had seemed a likely possibility after he had done some initial comparisons. All the data entered on the division's timekeeping and payroll system on the computer carried both the employee's name and his employee number. Manually, though, all processing and controls were based on the employee's name alone, since the division was small and everyone was known to everyone else. The reverse was not true for the computerized system, however. All the processing was done by numbers. The computer even used numbers, without any reference to employees' names, to look up names and addresses to print payroll checks.

Anyone with larcenous intent who understood the system could have used it in several fashions to feather his or her own nest, Cramer knew. He recalled one case in Harrisburg, Pennsylvania, where the payroll supervisor had filled out fake overtime forms for employees, but entered his own employee number in the computer.

However, Mays had not been sticking his hand into the Coca-Cola cookie jar through that particular loophole. Cramer was back at square one.

Chapter 3

What the use of fingerprints was to the 19th century and DNA analysis was to the 20th, forensic accounting will be to the 21st century.

> Gordon Brown, then
> Chancellor of the Exchequer,
> 10 October 2006

The crystal octagon continued its halting but unvarying revolutions. Ninety degrees, then a pause while a right index finger absently stroked the chilled dew from the sloping facet of the glass. About every revolution and a half, the glass rose, tilted a fraction of Pepsi across the waiting lips, and then descended to resume the circling libational ballet that had begun almost an hour before. Although he would not tell his current employer, he liked archrival Pepsi better than Coke.

Lenny Cramer was in one of his famous abstracted moods, what Becc called his "terminal trances," oblivious to all around him. Not that there was that much to which to be oblivious. Becc had already gone to bed, and Cramer had never been much of one for background music or television. The house was quiet, with only the muted rumble of the Roswell Road traffic intruding on its silence. He was breaking his personal rule, never to drink caffeine after 9:00 in the evening. Three hours from now he would be wide-awake. For some reason he remembered the fact that a bottle of soda contains approximately one-fourth the amount of caffeine as a cup of brewed coffee, and about one-third that of tea.

He was mulling over the day's events. The Coca-Cola investigation was not going badly. By any measure, it was far too early to make that judgment. But Cramer did want to wrap the project up with a minimum of expense to his client. He wanted the company's divisional superintendent as a reference later, and the quicker he could get to the bottom of matters at the soft-drink company, the greater the likelihood of a glowing reference. That meant either he needed a lot of luck in identifying any misuse or misappropriation of funds, or he needed to zero in on the process that was being misused. Lenny Cramer had never been one to trust anything to luck. That left only one other alternative—raw intelligence. Thus, the deep contemplation.

Two possible scams he had already eliminated in the past hour. One was the Salami technique. Though not particularly sophisticated, this technique had proved effective many times for the larcenously inclined, Cramer knew. Someone with appropriate access randomly reduces accounts by a tiny fraction of what each totals, normally 10 to 15 cents, and reallocates the funds to another account within the system. The money is then drawn down. Because the funds are simply rearranged within the system, no controls are breached. The losses to each account are so minimal they either go unnoticed or unreported. Such scams work moderately well with large numbers of accounts held by many people, as in the banking system. The scam also could work internally with one corporation, if inventories were the salami being sliced, rather than funds. In the case of Coke's international division, though, Cramer knew that the number of accounts was insufficient to generate any substantial amount of cash, even if someone was using the Salami technique. The same was true of inventory salami-slicing. About all a thief could get would be enough Cokes to supply a middle-sized fourth of July party.

The other technique he was confident could be eliminated was the Round-down. Such schemes required great numbers of accounts that involved percentage chargeables or payables, such as credit cards or savings accounts. Frequently, when a sum is multiplied by the required percentage, the result is less than a full cent. In round-downs, the swindler randomly chooses a number of the accounts to round down to the nearest cent. The fraction of a cent then goes into a separate account to which he has access. The customer loses nothing, since he would not have received the fraction of a cent anyway, and he is never the wiser. With large numbers of accounts, the technique can add up to large sums being misappropriated. But, just as in the salami technique, Coke simply did not have the volume of accounts required for such a scam to work.

"No, the fraudulent technique had to be something else, something quite simple and direct, probably some weekly or monthly expense incurred by the division that would be obvious once spotted," thought Cramer. "Possibly the scheme is one that would surface in a full-scale audit, but I have to find it a lot quicker than that. He knew that like rust, fraud never sleeps."

The glass paused midway in one of its upward swings, then slowly drifted downward again. The revolutions stopped, then resumed again abruptly for a 180-degree turn before the glass swiftly made a full trip back up. Cramer, the faraway look vanished, swished down the last of the Pepsi, then strode to the sink and dumped the ice. With a smile of obvious satisfaction, he flipped off the light on the way to his bedroom for what he wished would be a night of sound sleep.

* * *

Posey was right. Jeanne Saxet knew her business, and just about everybody else's, too.

"Jeanne, do all the employees of the international division work here in Atlanta?" Cramer asked as soon as he was settled into his temporary office the next morning.

"Oh, no," the secretary quickly replied. "We have quite a few who work elsewhere. There are several in New York, for example, who work out of the offices of another Coke division there, though we have jurisdiction over them. There is a small branch in Los Angeles that takes care of much of the Asian market. And, of course, at any given time we'll have operatives in several foreign locations, establishing new markets. Those are permanently assigned to this office, though they may stay out-of-country for as much as a year or two."

"The New York and L.A. staff ... they're permanently assigned there?" Cramer asked. "How are they paid?"

"By bank transfer, I think, in every case," Jeanne said.

"How about expenses? Do they have expense accounts? If they do, how are they paid?"

"Now that you ask, I'm not sure how they're paid," the secretary replied thoughtfully. "I know they each send in an accounting each month. I've seen those. But I'm not sure exactly how payment is handled."

"Tell you what, Jeanne, please pull me a hard copy of the New York and L.A. staff roster. Then let's take a look at their last few expense accounts," Cramer said. It was difficult to keep the edge of excitement from his voice.

Within 15 minutes, the auditor's suspicions had been confirmed. As noon approached, he called Posey and suggested they have lunch together.

* * *

"It was simple, once I thought about it," Cramer told the Coke executive as they nibbled at their salads. "It all tied back to your accounting system. Payables to the staff … uh salary and expenses … are all processed by name, though the employee number appears on the forms. But for the computer bookkeeping, it's all done by number. So, Mays has been submitting phony expense forms for the staffers in New York and Los Angeles. When it goes on the computer, though, he inserts his employee number. The funds have been deposited directly into a separate bank account he established.

"Since employees don't get W-2 forms or a Form 1099 for out-of-pocket expenses they are reimbursed, they were never aware of the scam. He was issuing two checks, one to the employee for the legitimate expenses and one to him that was direct-deposited. Mays is randomly rotating the bogus expense checks among the various out-of-town staffers. Not too sophisticated, but effective for a time."

"Good job, Lenny," Posey said enthusiastically. "I knew we'd gotten the right accountant. Any idea how much he's taken?"

"Not yet, but you're not going to be looking at any losses that will shake Coca-Cola to its fiscal foundations," Cramer replied. "This scheme is really penny-ante stuff. The most I've found so far, going back about three months, is six or seven hundred dollars a month.

The final take really depends on how long it's been going on. That isn't really the question, though."

"No?" Posey asked, puzzled. "What else is there?"

"Well," Cramer went on, choosing his word carefully. "You can cure this problem easily, just by getting rid of Mays. And you can probably prevent a recurrence of this particular scam by changing your accounting procedures slightly. One way to do that, for example, is for all computer accounting procedures to append to each employee's number the first three letters of his surname. That way it's readily apparent to anyone who's looking, that something is awry. What bothers me is that we've caught a greedy little guppy, but you may be letting sharks into the swimming pool."

"What do you mean?" Posey asked.

"Well ... Will, I hope you know me well enough to know that I'm not going to start crying 'Wolf' just to generate a little business. But your computer security is awfully loose. There have been a couple of times in the past few days that I've been astonished at the virtually unrestricted access that Jeanne has had, for example ... don't get me wrong.

I'm not saying Jeanne has done anything wrong, or has even thought about it, for that matter. She seems to be the epitome of the dedicated, loyal, and totally honest employee. But with all the data locked up in your computer, access should be tightly controlled. It should be almost like military secrets, on a 'need-to-know' basis."

"So what do you suggest?" Posey asked.

"I think you need to have someone with more expertise than me take a look at what you're doing, and see where things need to be tightened up. I'm not trying to expand the scope of what you hired me to do just to keep drawing my consultation fee. Believe me, there's a lot of potential for some major harm."

"Certainly I believe you," Posey said with a grin. "I've never doubted you ever since that time you told me you could talk that damned parakeet of mine down out of a tree after he escaped—and you did it."

"I never did tell you about the bird seed I had in the rim of my hat, did I?" Cramer chuckled.

"No, you didn't," Posey said, loosing an explosive laugh. "And for years I've been telling that story, about my friend with the mystical way with animals. You're nothing but a lousy con man yourself. Now tell me: What're you on to here? What exactly do you want us to do? Remember, that's Uncle Jemima's jurisdiction ... who, now that I think about it ... is on vacation for a couple of weeks."

"I took the liberty of making a call this morning to a professor at Wharton who's a specialist in computer auditing techniques. He's got a grad student who has already earned his CPA, and has taken off a semester before he starts on his dissertation that focuses on expert systems. This grad student is right here in Atlanta. My friend said if anyone can find which buttons are available to be pushed by the wrong people, it's this fellow. His name's Beauregard Duncan. They call him 'Slam' Duncan, though why I don't know. Anyway, I thought you might be interested in talking to him, and having him take a look at the security controls you have. He may save you some major headaches down the road."

"I certainly like the idea," Posey said thoughtfully. "Of course, we'll have to take it up with Joe. Meanwhile, these steaks deserve something better than to be ignored."

Chapter 4

Attestation standards generally provide for three types of engagements: examination, review, and agreed-upon procedures. The AICPA's Statements on Standards for Attestation Engagements (SSAEs) provide additional guidance on these types of engagements. The PCAOB adopted the SSAEs on an interim basis in April 2003.

—W.F.Messier, Jr.
Steven Glover
D.F. Prawitt

"So ... what does it boil down to? On how long a ride have we been taken?" Joe impaled Cramer and Posey with one of his patented piercing gazes.

"I don't think I've ever known anyone who could simultaneously look determined and sound resigned," Cramer thought to himself. "Of course, I don't guess I've known too many guys who've been in his shoes, either, looking at their career spiraling down the toilet because they couldn't stay faithful to a lifelong marital commitment. Even a non-religious person should know there's an ultimate price to pay for immorality."

"Not nearly as bad as it could be, Joe," Posey responded. "It looks like Dan Mays has been massaging the expense reports of the people in the New York and L.A. offices for about two and a half years now, submitting fake expense reports and having the payments deposited into an account at a Bank of America branch in Fairburn. Best Lenny can make out, he's snared about $119,000."

"Is he nailed?" Joe demanded. Posey turned to Cramer.

"Oh, yes, I don't think there's any question about that," Cramer interposed. "We've got the account number at the Fairburn branch, where he's been making the deposits. Shouldn't be difficult at all to establish whose account it is, even if he's been using an assumed name. He's also left a wide paper trail. Some of the expense reports are obvious forgeries, once you start looking for them. I don't think there's going to be much difficulty at all in getting a conviction."

"Conviction?" Joe's voice rose a quarter-register. "Uh, well, uh, yes, that's one of the alternatives we'll have to examine, of course. Considering the nature of the case, though, we'll also have to take a look at whether it's in the company's best interest to pursue a criminal action. You know ... there are a couple of considerations. The lost time from work that the witnesses would have, and the bad publicity when an employee is publicly identified as a thief are factors to consider. Maybe it's best just to get rid of Mays and write off the loss. Besides, we don't want to give anybody else any ideas, now, do we?"

Cramer and Posey glanced furtively at each other. "Yes, Will," Cramer thought, "I'm reading his mind just like you. If Joe tries to ship Mays off to jail, his wife is going to raise cane, and one of the first things that she's going to raise cane about is the little fling she had with the boss. That'll cost Joe not only his job, but his wife. He's in a sticky wicket. On the other hand, if he just lets the guy know what he has, he can force him to resign, get the wife transferred to another division, and let the ex-girlfriend know that if their previous cozy relationship ever surfaces, her husband is headed downriver to be tailored for a striped suit. He can do it under the guise of avoiding some bad press for the company. Nice finesse."

"Oh, I agree, Joe," Posey said. "One thing we don't want bandied around is that it's easy to embezzle Coke's hard-earned money."

"Cramer also suggests that we can use the Form 1099 technique to try to get the money back from Mays. Since the embezzled money is taxable income, we can explain to Mays that we will be forced to send a Form 1099 to the IRS if Mays does not sign an installment obligation to pay the money back."

"I like that idea, Cramer." Joe broke a smile. "Do it."

"Along those lines, Cramer had some interesting observations the other day. He seems to think that maybe we ought to take a closer look at all our computer security. Appears that it's not at all difficult for people to get sticky fingers, as lax as the Syrup Set has been in handling the computer processing."

"You dangle the bait so enticingly," Cramer thought, "letting Joe know that maybe his old foe Uncle Jemima has a chink in his corporate armor."

"How does that affect us?" Joe asked. "That's Jemima Clifford's department. If he's got a problem, then we'll need to let him know about it."

"It was almost like taking a dose of castor oil for him to say that," Cramer thought. "These two really don't like each other. So let's see how far he's willing to go with this game of corporate one-up-manship."

"We don't know that there are any problems, Joe. Or at least any problems that have resulted in any other losses. What Lenny tells me, though, is that the whole system lacks any kind of meaningful security. If that's the situation, then it is our business. We've got data on that system that can't be replaced. And data that we don't want to fall into the wrong hands. Lenny tells me he can get someone in for a few weeks, let him take a look at the access we have to the system, and determine if it's too unrestricted. There'd be almost no contact with the other division. They wouldn't even have to know we're doing it. I know it would be best to wait till Uncle Jemima … uh, Jemima … is back from his vacation, but Lenny tells me this fellow is the best, and he's only going to be available for a few weeks. He's out of Philadelphia, and as I understand it, he is here to visit his folks. If anything comes of it, we'll, of course, kick it over to Jemima immediately."

"You are smooth, Will, you silver-tongued rascal," Cramer thought admiringly. "I never knew you had it in you to play these games so skillfully. He's here to see his folks, all right—for four months. Without ever saying so, you've let Joe know he can turn this debacle with Mays into a star in his crown, if he can uncover some real serious security problems in the other division. At the same time, if things are as loose over there as they seem to be with the computer system, Joe can slap it to a corporate rival like a spoiled mackerel right in the face. And he can have it all in place before Uncle Jemima even gets back into town and gets wind of anything. Neat. Real neat."

Cramer watched with amusement as Joe almost visibly went through the same mental scenario. Finally, the division chief unfolded his hands and stood up.

"Okay, Will, whatever you think is best. Just don't get in anybody's hair over there on the Syrup side, and for goodness sake don't give anybody the idea we think they're running a sloppy operation. Any accessing you do, I want it to be confined as far as possible to those programs we're supposed to be screwing around with, not the Syrup Set's database. And Lenny, I don't want anybody planning to buy their vacation cottage with Coca-Cola auditing fees. Keep the time down, and keep the fees reasonable. We pay E&Y a fortune. I've got to get to a meeting downtown at Sun Trust, but I want to hear from you in a couple of days."

Turning to Will, Joe said, "Get Mays out of the office till 4 o'clock today. Send him on whatever errands you can find, and have Jeanne cut his final paycheck. Give him his accrued vacation, but no severance pay. Get his password out of our computer system now. I don't want him to do any more damage. We'll wrap up any loose ends later, but at 4 o'clock I want him and you in my office so I can personally fire him. Run me a copy of several of those forged expense accounts, too. Just to make sure we got him cold, call one of the people in L.A. and one in New York on the latest expense accounts. Tell 'em there's been some kind of screw-up down here. Go over their original submission, and verify that the bogus expenses were never incurred. Remember, 4 o'clock, with his final paycheck ready. That scheming scumbag."

"One other thing. Check the job board. See what job is available in Connie Mays' pay bracket for which she qualifies. I sure don't want a disgruntled wife making waves in my division."

As Cramer left the office, he noticed a brightly colored book on Joe's desk. It was entitled *Coca-Cola Superstar*, by Fiora S. Palazzini.

* * *

"May I speak to Mr. Duncan, please?" Cramer asked.

"Sure. Take your choice," the voice replied, too jauntily for Cramer's taste. "You want a Mr. Duncan who's drawing Social Security, a Mr. Duncan who right now is drawing a beer—that's me—or a Mr. Duncan who's drawing flies, while he's trying to get a tan in the back yard? That's my little brother, bless his pea-pickin' soul, and curse his pluperfect pectorals."

"Uh, Mr. Beauregard Duncan. From Wharton."

"You got him. What can I do for you?"

"This is Lenny Cramer. I'm a CPA. I was on the faculty at Wharton until recently. Dr. Nelson suggested I get in touch with you about a forensic audit I'm involved in here in Atlanta."

"How's Dr. Nelson doing? Did he get his office straightened out after setting fire to the wastebasket with his pipe?" Duncan asked.

"Yes, he's got everything back into shape again. Not much damage, except to a few books." Cramer, normally not one to make snap judgments, made an exception in this case. He decided he liked neither this impudent young man nor the prospect of working with him. He was on the verge of terminating the conversation when two thoughts, tumbling over each other for acknowledgment, stopped him. First was memory of Nelson's ringing recommendation of Duncan. "The absolute best at wringing dirty laundry out of a computer." The second was the recollection that Joe had placed him on a short lease, time-wise. The likelihood of finding anybody truly qualified in so short of time was slim, especially considering the nature of the job.

"Look, Mr. Duncan, I know …"

"Call me Slam, please," Duncan interrupted. "My folks didn't have any boy-children they gave the first name of 'Mr.' to."

"I know this is short notice," Cramer continued, unable to bring himself to be so familiar as to use a nickname. "But I wonder if you could possibly drop by my office in Sandy Springs this evening about 5:30? I'd like to talk to you about the investigative audit I'm on. It shouldn't take but half an hour or so, and I'll be happy to pay your regular consultation fee."

"Sure. Just give me the address. I'm just a little south of the loop, so it won't take me long at all."

* * *

Cramer was just opening the door to his office when he was startled by a motorcycle careening into the driveway. Cramer did not ride motorcycles. He did not *like* motorcycles, viewing them with the same distaste that he had for hot rods, dune buggies, and the many other diverse manifestations of the inexplicable compulsion some people have to turn perfectly reasonable vehicles of transport into weird, uncomfortable, unsightly and frequently noisy contraptions. He instantly disliked this motorcycle more than most, since it sported an extended fork that tilted the bike so much it seemed someone had tried to turn the motorcycle into a mobile isosceles triangle. The rider astride the motorcycle seemed to have legs even longer than the fork that stretched interminably in front of the handlebars. He virtually undulated off the motorcycle and removed his helmet, revealing a shock of straight black hair as thick as a brand-new mop.

"Lenny Cramer? I'm Slam Duncan." The hand that engulfed Cramer's felt like it was broad enough to pick up a 55-gallon drum. The owner of the hand appeared to be approximately as tall as a moderate-sized New England lighthouse.

"Yes, I'm Dr. Cramer, of course. Glad to meet you." Cramer mentally kicked himself as he extracted his hand from the wraparound grip. He never used the "Dr." People who insisted on announcing their academic credentials right off irritated him. But so did this six-foot-six apparition in front of him, and even without realizing it he wanted to put some distance between himself and Duncan. "Come on in. I told my secretary to make a pot of coffee before she left. Let's see if she did."

"I'll pass on the coffee, thanks. Never drink anything that looks like it's made of floorsweep, I say. But you go ahead."

"I will, thank you. Why don't you grab a chair, and I'll explain to you the possible assignment." Cramer thought grimly, "I am not going to be a happy camper for the next few days." With his cup of coffee and with resignation, he put aside his distaste, and began briefing Duncan on the situation, leaving out any details on the office in-fighting and any references to Joe's indiscretions. Duncan sat quietly, listening intently as he unconsciously pulled at a forelock of long black hair. Cramer was surprised, when he got to the scam Mays had been pulling, at how quickly Duncan caught on. In fact, he had interrupted to ask if the expense accounts had been standing in the academic accounting profession. Good old solid, plodding Will, who'd wrangled Cramer's new clinical teaching post at Georgia State University for the fall, who had found the small bungalow he and Rebecca would be renting, along with the small office where Cramer would set up shop. Will had already gotten him his first commission, a small auditing job at the Coca-Cola division where Will worked in the overseas development division.

Ernst & Young LLP was Coke's independent auditor who performed its yearly financial statement audit. The purpose of a financial statement audit is to provide an opinion of the fairness of the statements, as to conformity with generally accepted accounting principles (GAAP). Will wanted Cramer to perform a forensic audit without the word getting out to many people. The job wasn't exactly hush-hush, as Cramer understood it, but Will did want the project kept quiet. The job was small potatoes compared to the not-so-distant days when Cramer was a consultant to major international corporations, but Cramer was grateful both for the work and for the confidence his friend had shown in him.

"We'd better get started if we're going to see everything at Stone Mountain before the light show tonight," Cramer told his daughter as he beckoned for the check. The two had planned to take in the huge granite mountain east of Atlanta as their one day of fun before buckling down for a couple of weeks of getting their new home into shape. Atlanta's other attractions — the Cyclorama, the zoo, the High Museum, the state Capitol — would have to wait until later. Cramer wanted to give his daughter at least a taste of the delights the Southern metropolis held, and Stone Mountain seemed to be the best way to do that.

His judgment turned out to be eminently correct. After a day of ogling the huge carving of Southern heroes Robert E. Lee, Stonewall Jackson, and Jefferson Davis that graced the side of the mountain, riding the train, visiting the game ranch and old car museum, and oohing at the laser light show, the two returned to their hotel that night tired but enthusiastic over what their new home held in store. Cramer was amused and grateful, but just a little wistful, when he noticed how much Becc's attitude toward the move improved when she met a group of teenage boys at the Stone Mountain park lake, where they relaxed with a dip in the cool water for an hour or two.

"I guess a parent hasn't done his job right if he doesn't eventually render himself unnecessary," Cramer mused before he drifted off to sleep. "But that doesn't make it any easier."

* * *

The next few days were a blur of scrubbing, sweeping, vacuuming, mopping, waxing, washing windows, moving furniture, moving it back again, hanging pictures, painting, mowing, pulling weeds, and all the other multitudinous tasks involved in setting up housekeeping. The bungalow had been unoccupied for the past year and half while it was tied up in an estate, and the long vacancy showed. Cobwebs seemed to flourish more in the South than the North, Cramer noted. Rebecca worked right beside him without complaining, but Cramer knew it was an inauspicious introduction to her new home, and he made it a point to give her frequent breaks while he himself kept working away.

The house was smaller than either he or Becc were accustomed to, and Cramer didn't care much for the idea of renting. It wasn't that he couldn't afford to buy. Cramer was far from being on the dole. But with the uncertainties of starting a new firm in a new city, he thought it best to husband his resources for a year or two. Besides, he wanted the opportunity to get to know Atlanta and environs before settling down in a permanent residence. There would be plenty of time to buy after the Philadelphia place sold. The tax code allows a single homeowner to exclude up to $250,000 of realized gain on the sale of his home in Philadelphia even if he did not buy a new home.

Several times Cramer called a halt while he went to his nearby office. That, too, had to be shaped up, and Cramer didn't have the heart to ask for Becc's help. The same van that had brought the Cramer household goods had brought enough of the furnishings from his former office in Philadelphia to equip the new quarters in Atlanta. Though he wasn't confronted with the same house-cleaning chores that awaited him at home, Cramer still had to interview for a secretary, get his telephones hooked up, and unpack checked even before Cramer got around to telling him exactly what the scam had been. Then he had virtually barraged Cramer with questions about the division's computer security, methods of access, and so on, till finally the CPA had to call a halt. He was astonished to discover, on checking his watch, that almost three hours had passed.

This giant may be an odd duck, but he's no quack. He felt a bit more comfortable as he watched the lanky rider roar off, now officially associated in the operational-type audit.

* * *

That evening at home Cramer began working on his auditing lecture notes. He would be teaching a basic auditing course at Georgia State in the fall, and he wanted to use E&Y's audit report of Coca-Cola as a handout. E&Y, of course, had issued the standard unqualified opinion. An *unqualified* opinion gives a company a clean bill of health, but the accounting profession takes the position that a search for *defalcations* in financial statements requires audit procedures far beyond those normally used in a financial statement audit.

Cramer knew that conditions may prevent an auditor from following generally accepted auditing standards or the auditors might find something during the audit to stop them from reporting that the financial statements are fair in accordance with GAAP. Thus, three other types of reports may be issued: a qualified opinion, a disclaimer, or an adverse opinion.

Two reasons may cause an auditor to issue a *qualified* opinion. First, something may prevent an auditor from performing all of the necessary audit procedures (e.g. the auditor being unable to examine records of a foreign subsidiary or to observe the inventory count). This first reason is referred to as a scope limitation. Second, the auditor may decide that the company did not follow GAAP (e.g., the company improperly computing the value of inventory).

When financial statements are not presented fairly in accordance with GAAP, an auditor will issue an adverse or qualified opinion. Whether to use a qualified or adverse opinion depends on the extent to which the departure from GAAP standards affects the overall financial statements. An adverse opinion is rare. On the other hand, when an auditor lacks the knowledge to form any opinion on the financial statements, a disclaimer opinion is appropriate. A disclaimer type of opinion is used when the auditor lacks sufficient evidence to form an opinion. For example, an auditor may be prevented from completing a substantial portion of an audit.

Cramer read through the audit opinion and the auditor's opinion as to the Coke's internal controls. He underlined some important information, especially the information about the PCAOB.

The Sarbanes-Oxley Act of 2002 created a new, five-member oversight group called the Public Company Accounting Oversight Board (PCAOB). This group is a strong, independent, and full-time oversight board with broad authority to regulate auditors of public companies, set auditing standards, and investigate violations. Only two of its members can be or have been CPAs. The Board is subject to SEC review and establishes auditing, quality control, ethics, and independence standards for public company auditors. The PCAOB's mission is to protect investors in U.S. securities markets and to further the public interest by ensuring that public company financial statements are audited according to the highest standards of quality, independence, and ethics. The Board is funded by fees from public companies.

The PCAOB is empowered to set accounting standards that establish auditing, quality control and ethical standards for accountants. The Board also is empowered to adopt or amend standards issued or recommended by private accounting industry groups or to adopt its own standards independent of such private industry standards or recommendations. Auditing Standards have been historically created by the AICPA and many had thought that the PCAOB would delegate its authority to set standards to the AICPA. However, the Board is setting standards itself. Because the Board is setting standards, auditors are seeing many more changes in auditing standards.

The Sarbanes-Oxley Act and SAS No. 99 put pressure on management, audit committees, chief executives, CFOs, external accountants, and internal auditors to incorporate forensic accounting techniques into their jobs. Now CEOs and CFOs must certify in each 10-K and 10-Q that the signing officer has reviewed the report, and state that based upon the officer's knowledge there are no material misstatements or omissions and the financial statements fairly represent the financial condition and results of operations.

One could argue that before Enron and the other scandals surfaced, no one accepted ultimate responsibility for finding fraud. Independent auditors disclaim such responsibility in their engagement letters. Internal auditors put disclaimers in their charters. Management looked to audit committees. Audit committees looked to independent auditors. Independent auditors looked to management. Were it not for the phenomenal amount of investment funds and jobs lost by innocent individuals, the whole business would remind one of the "Who's on first" classic comedy routine.

Will fraud detection now become primarily the responsibility of forensic accountants? Will there be forensic sleuths hired every year for the annual audit or carried on staff? Will forensic accountants have a special role in each internal audit function? Will audit committees insist on the services of a forensic accountant? The answer: No one really knows.

The approach up until now based on Sarbanes-Oxley is to make *everyone* responsible for fighting fraud by increasing all parties' responsibilities for uncovering such fraud in every direction at every step in the process.

Since management may override controls, substantive analytical procedures alone are not well suited for detecting fraud. The PCAOB indicates that an auditor's substantive procedures must include reconciling the financial statements to the accounting records. Such substantive procedures also must include reconciling the financial statements to the accounting records. The auditor's substantive procedures also should include examining material adjustments made during the course of preparing the financial statements, especially so-called "top-drawer" entries made by management near year-end. Also, other auditing standards require auditors to perform specific tests of details in the financial statement audit.

For example, AU Sec. 316 requires an auditor to perform tests of detail to further address the risk of management override, whether or not a specific risk of fraud has been identified. Also, AU Sec. 330 states that there is a presumption that the auditor will request the confirmation of accounts receivable. Finally, AU Sec. 331 states that observation of inventories is a generally accepted procedure and that the auditor who issues an opinion without this procedure "has the burden of justifying the opinion expressed."

The adoption of SAS No. 99 by the Auditing Standards Board (ASB) was an attempt to close the so-called expectation gap between professional standards and the belief of the outside world that the role of auditors is to find fraud. Now external auditors must gather information needed to identify risks of material misstatements due to fraud, assess these risks, and respond to the results.

A fraud audit is a separate job from a financial statement audit. In a typical forensic audit, there is an allegation of fraud or fraud has already been discovered. The CPA firm is called in as a consultant to gather evidence or to act as an expert witness with respect to legal proceedings relating to the fraud.

As Cramer reviewed the financial reports, he underlined some important information for his students.

REPORT OF MANAGEMENT ON INTERNAL CONTROL OVER FINANCIAL REPORTING
The Coca-Cola Company and Subsidiaries

Management of the Company is responsible for the preparation and integrity of the consolidated financial statements appearing in our annual report on Form 10-K. The financial statements were prepared in conformity with generally accepted accounting principles appropriate in the circumstances and, accordingly, include certain amounts based on our best judgments and estimates. Financial information in this annual report on Form 10-K is consistent with that in the financial statements.

Management of the Company is responsible for establishing and maintaining adequate internal control over financial reporting as such term is defined in Rule 13a-15(f) under the Securities Exchange Act of 1934 ("Exchange Act"). The Company's internal control over financial reporting is designed to provide reasonable assurance regarding the reliability of financial reporting and the preparation of the consolidated financial statements. Our internal control over financial reporting is supported by a program of internal audits and appropriate reviews by management, written policies and guidelines, careful selection and training of qualified personnel and a written Code of Business Conduct adopted by our Company's Board of Directors, applicable to all officers and employees of our Company and subsidiaries. In addition, our Company's Board of Directors adopted a written Code of Business Conduct for Non-Employee Directors which reflects the same principles and values as our Code of Business Conduct for officers and employees but focuses on matters of most relevance to non-employee Directors.

Because of its inherent limitations, internal control over financial reporting may not prevent or detect misstatements and, even when determined to be effective, can only provide reasonable assurance with respect to financial statement preparation and presentation. Also, projections of any evaluation of effectiveness to future periods are subject to the risk that controls may become inadequate because of changes in conditions, or that the degree of compliance with the policies or procedures may deteriorate.

The Audit Committee of our Company's Board of Directors, composed solely of Directors who are independent in accordance with the requirements of the New York Stock Exchange listing standards, the Exchange Act and the Company's Corporate Governance Guidelines, meets with the independent auditors, management and internal auditors periodically to discuss internal control over financial reporting and auditing and financial reporting matters. The Audit Committee reviews with the independent auditors the scope and results of the audit effort. The Audit Committee also meets periodically with the independent auditors and the chief internal auditor without management present to ensure that the independent auditors and the chief internal auditor have free access to the Audit Committee. Our Audit Committee's Report can be found in the Company's 2009 Proxy Statement.

Management assessed the effectiveness of the Company's internal control over financial reporting as of December 31, 2008. In making this assessment, management used the criteria set forth by the Committee of Sponsoring Organizations of the Treadway Commission (COSO) in Internal Control-Integrated Framework. Based on our assessment, management believes that the Company maintained effective internal control over financial reporting as of December 31, 2008.

The Company's independent auditors, Ernst & Young LLP, a registered public accounting firm, are appointed by the Audit Committee of the Company's Board of Directors, subject to ratification by our Company's shareowners. Ernst & Young LLP has audited and reported on the consolidated financial statements of The Coca-Cola Company and subsidiaries and the Company's internal control over financial reporting. The reports of the independent auditors are contained in this annual report.

Muhtar Kent Harry,
President and Chief Executive Officer
February 26, 2009

L. Anderson,
Vice President and Controller
February 26, 2009

Gary P. Fayard
Executive Vice President and Chief Financial Officer
February 26, 2009

Report of Independent Registered
Public Accounting Firm
Board of Directors and Shareowners
The Coca-Cola Company

We have audited the accompanying consolidated balance sheets of The Coca-Cola Company and subsidiaries as of December 31, 2008 and 2007, and the related consolidated statements of income, shareowners' equity, and cash flows for each of the three years in the period ended December 31, 2008. These financial statements are the responsibility of the Company's management. Our responsibility is to express an opinion on these financial statements based on our audits.

We conducted our audits in accordance with the standards of the Public Company Accounting Oversight Board (United States). Those standards require that we plan and perform the audit to obtain reasonable assurance about whether the financial statements are free of material misstatement. An audit includes examining, on a test basis, evidence supporting the amounts and disclosures in the financial statements. An audit also includes assessing the accounting principles used and significant estimates made by management, as well as evaluating the overall financial statement presentation. We believe that our audits provide a reasonable basis for our opinion.

In our opinion, the financial statements referred to above present fairly, in all material respects, the consolidated financial position of The Coca-Cola Company and subsidiaries at December 31, 2008 and 2007, and the consolidated results of their operations and their cash flows for each of the three years in the period ended December 31, 2008, in conformity with U.S. generally accepted accounting principles.

As discussed in Notes 1 and 17 to the consolidated financial statements, in 2007 the Company adopted FASB

Interpretation No. 48 related to accounting for uncertainty in income taxes. Also as discussed in Notes 1 and 16 to the consolidated financial statements, in 2006 the Company adopted SFAS No. 158 related to defined benefit pension and other postretirement plans.

We also have audited, in accordance with the standards of the Public Company Accounting Oversight Board (United States), The Coca-Cola Company's internal control over financial reporting as of December 31, 2008, based on criteria established in Internal Control-Integrated Framework issued by the Committee of Sponsoring Organizations of the Treadway Commission and our report dated February 26, 2009 expressed an unqualified opinion thereon.

Ernst & Young LLP
Atlanta, Georgia
February 26, 2009

Report of Independent Registered Public Accounting Firm on Internal Control Over Financial Reporting
Board of Directors and Shareowners
The Coca-Cola Company

We have audited The Coca-Cola Company's internal control over financial reporting as of December 31, 2008, based on criteria established in Internal Control-Integrated Framework issued by the Committee of Sponsoring Organizations of the Treadway Commission (the COSO criteria). The Coca-Cola Company's management is responsible for maintaining effective internal control over financial reporting, and for its assessment of the effectiveness of internal control over financial reporting included in the accompanying Report of Management on Internal Control Over Financial Reporting. Our responsibility is to express an opinion on the Company's internal control over financial reporting based on our audit.

We conducted our audit in accordance with the standards of the Public Company Accounting Oversight Board (United States). Those standards require that we plan and perform the audit to obtain reasonable assurance about whether effective internal control over financial reporting was maintained in all material respects. Our audit included obtaining an understanding of internal control over financial reporting, assessing the risk that a material weakness exists, testing and evaluating the design and operating effectiveness of internal control based on the assessed risk, and performing such other procedures as we considered necessary in the circumstances. We believe that our audit provides a reasonable basis for our opinion.

A company's internal control over financial reporting is a process designed to provide reasonable assurance regarding the reliability of financial reporting and the preparation of financial statements for external purposes in accordance with generally accepted accounting principles. A company's internal control over financial reporting includes those policies and procedures that (1) pertain to the maintenance of records that, in reasonable detail, accurately and fairly reflect the transactions and dispositions of the assets of the company;

(2) provide reasonable assurance that transactions are recorded as necessary to permit preparation of financial statements in accordance with generally accepted accounting principles, and that receipts and expenditures of the company are being made only in accordance with authorizations of management and directors of the company; and (3) provide reasonable assurance regarding prevention or timely detection of unauthorized acquisition, use, or disposition of the company's assets that could have a material effect on the financial statements.

Because of its inherent limitations, internal control over financial reporting may not prevent or detect misstatements. Also, projections of any evaluation of effectiveness to future periods are subject to the risk that controls may become inadequate because of changes in conditions, or that the degree of compliance with the policies or procedures may deteriorate.

In our opinion, The Coca-Cola Company maintained, in all material respects, effective internal control over financial reporting as of December 31, 2008, based on the COSO criteria.

We also have audited, in accordance with the standards of the Public Company Accounting Oversight Board (United States), the consolidated balance sheets of The Coca-Cola Company and subsidiaries as of December 31, 2008 and 2007, and the related consolidated statements of income, shareowners' equity, and cash flows for each of the three years in the period ended December 31, 2008, and our report dated February 26, 2009 expressed an unqualified opinion thereon.

Ernst & Young LLP
Atlanta, Georgia
February 26, 2009

Chapter 5

Working papers should support an auditor's conclusions and, in an effort to promote understanding and minimize preparation time, should be clear, concise, and above all unambiguous. The sheer volume of working paper generated during an audit engagement is inconsequential; quantity is no substitute for quality.

— David N. Ricchiute

Cramer had made arrangements to meet Duncan at the Coca-Cola offices at 10 o'clock the next morning. After a late start getting Becc off to school, he dropped into his own office to see how things were going, and to pick up his briefcase. There he found Michele, who seemed to have things well in hand. There had been no telephone calls. The world of corporate Atlanta was taking its time in beating a path to his door, as he had resigned himself to expect.

Cramer was always amused when he drove into the Coke complex. There was a gate with a guard. No one could enter the premises without a name tag. In order for someone to visit, the guard had to call someone inside who gave permission for the person to enter. Lenny parked in the visitor's parking lot and went into the building. His red name tag rested prominently on his coat lapel. He stopped at a Coke machine on the ground floor and got a free diet Coke from the machine. Was it taxable? Oh, well, the Internal Revenue Service was *probably* not that picky.

In this area were various displays of Coca-Cola memorabilia, promotional advertisements, and other promotional merchandise. There was a Russell Yo-Yo made in the Philippines, evolution of the Coke can, 1929 cold-box, chronology of bottles used between

1900 and 1956, an 1891 Coca-Cola calendar, a syrup urn used as a premium in the 1890s, and more. The displays reminded him of a family vacation trip he had made long ago as a kid.

During one summer vacation, Cramer's family traveled to Vicksburg, Mississippi, to see its historical attractions, including the Biedenharn Candy Company and Museum of Coca-Cola Memorabilia. The museum was located in downtown Vicksburg on Washington Street. The restored building was where Coca-Cola was first bottled in 1894. The museum also featured Coca-Cola memorabilia, a 1900 soda fountain, and an 1890 candy store. One of his best memories of the museum, however, was not an historical artifact, but the delicious ice cream float and homemade candy that provided immense refreshment on a hot Mississippi summer day.

Cramer's parents both enjoyed historical attractions. His father was particularly fond of old battlefields. The Vicksburg National Military Park was renowned as one of the best. The 16-mile driving tour of the old battlefield was etched in his mind, even after all the intervening years. He remembered reading how two Missouri units, one Confederate and one Union, directly opposed one another at a strategic location. In a bloody battle, friend met friend, brother met brother, and neighbor met neighbor.

Later that morning, at precisely 10 o'clock, Cramer was closeted with Will Posey and Slam Duncan. Posey covered essentially the same ground Cramer had covered the night before, but not before exchanging a questioning glance at his old friend. Cramer simply shrugged slightly and raised his eyebrows a tad to show his own perplexity. After all, how do you explain a certified public accountant and alleged expert computer auditor who shows up for work toting a motorcycle helmet with a ninja warrior emblazoned across the back and wearing a Hawaiian flowered shirt that seemed to scream its colors. When Posey turned Cramer and Duncan over to his assistant, Laura Lee Bertone, Cramer could almost see the same thoughts bumping against each other in Posey's mind. They were no more numerous than his own.

"Tell me about your computer system. With so many subsidiaries in so many countries, how do you get the financial information to corporate headquarters?" Duncan asked abruptly.

Laura's first impression of Duncan wasn't flattering; he came across as arrogant. However, she good-naturedly responded to his question. "We fully utilize the advances made in computer and communication technology, unlike some companies."

"I assume you are talking about Pepsi."

"Sh-h-h-h," whispered Laura, with her index finger at her mouth. "Don't mention the P-word in here." She laughed.

"Actually, with fiber optic cables laid almost around the world, we can easily communicate through the Internet with all our international branches, customers, and suppliers. Since everyone uses HTML as a computer language, data can be transmitted and read on any computer anywhere. Plus, with standardized protocols that connect everyone's machines and software applications, I can just as easily communicate with a Coke employee in India as one in this building."

With a gleam in his eye, Duncan confessed to Cramer, "I think I'm in love. She's talking my language."

Turning back to Laura, Duncan asked, "I know that countries, including the U.S., are rapidly adopting International Financial Reporting Standards (IFRS). IFRS are principles-based and less descriptive, which will leave practitioners with a tremendous challenge in applying the rules. I believe there will be much more fraud and cooking the books as we switch to IFRS. However, what accounting practices do you have that are specific to the Coca-Cola Company?"

"Coke has a customized chart of accounts that defines our reporting needs. The chart has four sections: profit and loss, balance sheet, statistical accounts, and accounts for restatement or reclassification of the balance sheet and income statement account. Each remote location has a common framework under which to operate."

"Each location operates on inexpensive, compatible desktop PCs. The local accounting personnel enter the data into the PC. The local accountant is more familiar with its content." Laura paused.

"The local person translates their local currency data, such as pounds, into U.S. dollars. They report this data in both local currency and U.S. dollars, in similar format to be reviewed by headquarters' personnel. They—the local office—lock the data so that it cannot be changed at a future date and send it over a telecommunication network to headquarters. The main office can pull each location's financial information into its PC network."

"What security procedures do you employ?" Duncan asked.

"Hopefully a good, safe system. We have designated micro-computer rooms, security stations with steel doors, passwords ..."

"Passwords are notoriously ineffective as an access-control technique," Duncan almost shouted.

Ignoring him, Laura continued. "We have a user identity code and automatic password obsolescence on a short-time cycle basis. Further, to use the computer the valid user must be at a valid terminal on a valid day of the week. To stop an illegal person from accessing the computer while the legal person is also using the system, the computer checks and will disconnect both users. "

"How about cryptographic technology to protect your communication signals?"

"No. We are not NASA. We don't have any sensitive, classified governmental information in our system. The Coke formula is locked in a bank vault."

Duncan continued to probe. "What about separation of duties?"

"Data input and data output analyses are performed by different people. Library file procedures, programming, and actual system use are done by different people. We try to stop the fraud from occurring, but if fraud does occur, we can probably detect it."

Laura continued her discussion for about fifteen more minutes, and then Duncan was left to check the audit trail within the computer system. Duncan knew that a good audit trail was an essential control feature in a computer system. He checked the logs of the unsuccessful sign-on attempts and the unsuccessful access attempts. Duncan did not finish his review of the security controls until 7:10 that evening.

He made a note to check with Laura about Coke's contingency plans for a fire in the data processing center. Was most of the computer software stored in off-site fireproof safes? He knew that three out of four businesses hit by fire could not survive the 90 days necessary to rebuild a destroyed computer system. He had read of the fire that destroyed Worlco, Inc., a $25 million insurance and health care business. Due to planning, this company was able to resume collection and payments clerically and by a computer in a service bureau in a nearby city. What if a bursting pipe flooded the computer center? Suppose a disgruntled employee reformatted the hard disks?

* * *

"So ... how about we talk about this information over lunch?"

Laura Lee Bertone brushed back a lock of dark red hair and glanced up from the terminal. Duncan, whom she had worked with briefly during the past two days, was looming over her right elbow, holding a sheaf of papers.

"What's that?" she asked.

"The standardized immatrization synchronization for the primary syncolathe during the past quarter," Duncan replied.

"What?" Laura reached for the papers and quickly rifled through them. "What is this? A laundry bill? A book report? A magazine? This is a ... what did you call it?"

"The quarterly standardized immatrization synchronization for the primary syncolathe, or something like that. But you can call it anything you wish. Call it an old laundry bill. Call it a dog-eared copy of *Field & Stream*. What I'd rather do is call it an invitation to lunch at the Varsity. How about it?"

"Uh ... I guess so. Just one question: do we have to discuss how you clean your shirts?"

"We can talk about whatever you wish, dear lady, though I'd prefer to spend my time talking only about you."

Laura rolled her eyes upward and wondered if she was making a mistake.

Leaving the building together, Duncan guided Laura to their mode of transportation. "You're kidding. You jest. You can't be serious. That's what we're going to lunch on?" Laura looked at the motorcycle with dismay.

"Sure," Duncan replied.

"You really expect me to go to lunch on something out of a motorcycle gang flick? I can't do that."

"Sure you can. You're wearing slacks. I brought an extra helmet today, just for you. You'll like it. Naturally air-conditioned. Specially designed to make you feel you're a part of your environment. The ambiance of transportation at its absolute best."

"You're impossible, Slam," Laura laughed. "Okay, but get out of here quickly, will you, before somebody sees me? Please, don't try any loops or rolls, and take it slow. I value every single part of my anatomy just like it is. I don't want anything rearranged by somebody's bumper."

"A sentiment about your anatomy that I share completely," Slam said as he buckled on her helmet.

"The Varsity, over on North Avenue," Laura said. "Now that's a switch for a luncheon date. I haven't been there in ages, since I dated a Georgia Tech student years ago. Do they still have the famous Varsity 'V' sign?"

"You bet. We could try someplace else," Duncan said, though not with much enthusiasm.

"Oh, no, it's perfect," Laura responded quickly. "Nothing would go better with a Harley than a Varsity hot dog. We will eat inside, though. I'm putting my foot down on that. Besides, there's no place to hang a tray on this contraption."

"Whatever you say, m'lady. It does seem to me, though, that if you're going to be dining at the world's largest drive-in, you ought to be willing to experience it fully."

"I'm going to experience it fully from inside. And, I suspect my co-workers will experience a bit of it, too, when I get back to the office, because I'm going to get a double-dose of onions on my hot dog."

"Tell me about yourself," Duncan said after they'd received their hot dogs and fries and soft drinks. "Are you from here? Where did you go to school? How long have you been with Coke? Do you dye your eyes, or are they that color naturally? Can we do this tomorrow? When can I get you to pose for someone to paint your picture on my helmet?"

"Whoa, easy rider. One at a time, please. Yes, I'm from around here, sort of. I grew up in Savannah. My Dad died during my senior year in high school there. Mom managed to hang on until I graduated, but then we moved up here so I could go to school at Georgia State, and she could go to work in my uncle's business. He runs an auto parts store in Smyrna, and Mom was his office manager until she died several years ago. And although you didn't ask if I was funny as a child, I quote Ellen DeGeneres: 'well, no, I was an accountant.'"

"So you're a Georgia State alumna," Duncan commented. "Blue and white. Where is your blue pounce pin?"

"I went full-time for two and a half years. Then I had to go to work for a small CPA firm after Mom's death. Worked in accounting for three years and finished my degree at night school. Then I left the public accounting firm and came to Coke where I've been the last four years."

"Why did you stop the public accounting work?"

"I don't have time to tell you about the thousands of tax returns I completed. Auditing was more interesting, but what I really like is computer-related work. I have the opportunity to work more in the computer area here at Coke. Besides I was just plain tired of public accounting. Who knows why?"

Laura paused for a moment and then looked into Slam's eyes. "The eyes are my own, all the way. And I don't know about tomorrow. But if we do this again, I'll tell you right now we won't be moseying out on that piece of motorized mayhem out there. I don't exactly trust the driving skills of a guy whose helmet features a ninja warrior on the back. This adventure has been fun, but I'd like to get back to work now. I want to be off that motorcycle before the rest of the crew starts returning from what I suspect was a far saner lunch hour than I had."

Her smile, Duncan decided, showed she didn't mean a word of it.

Later that night Duncan thought about Laura. She had those eyes that were so hard to explain, like intangible assets. They were special, but not because they were so beautifully blue. They had those sparkles that tell *you* that she has a special interest in you. Yes, they were beautiful, but Laura's eyes were more. Her piercing gaze revealed a sharp mind working behind those eyes. She was attractive and intelligent, resourceful, and independent. Duncan felt a suspicion growing that he was in for some novel learning experiences with Laura—assuming that she was interested in him at all. Duncan realized he was scowling at himself, and wondered why.

Chapter 6

To protect against computer crimes, accountants should be accountants. There is no substitute for the old accounting nose, for the old investigative nose. You just have to do your homework.

—August Bequai

"Maybe I'm not supposed to ask this, but I'm going to anyway." The words were spoken lightly, as Laura tilted her head slightly to the left. The mannerism was one of the first things Slam had noticed about her. Never to the right, and never more than a little off the vertical. He found it charming.

Slam knew that some experts believe that a right-handed person tends to glance upward to their right before they tell a lie.

"Ask, m'lady," Slam replied. "Can I make ice cream sodas the old fashioned way. Sodas that would lure a leopard out of a tree? Do I sleep in socks? Does baldness run in my family? Are fatigues really my favorite apparel? Are most Mensa members egocentric insecure bores? Is there life after 30? Do I want to take you on a romantic cruise to the South Seas and live on coconuts and palm wine while the Polynesian breezes play harmony for the melodies my heart sings always when I am near you? The answer is yes, and yes, and yes again."

"The answer, m'lord, to all of the foregoing questions is that you can be the most exasperatingly, irreverent ball of blarney I've ever encountered."

"Ah ... You've found my one weakness. Flattery. Give me more."

"What are you and Dr. Cramer doing at the office? I know it's something out of the ordinary. You're in the office all day long, and it has been a couple of weeks now. What's going on? Has somebody been embezzling money, or something like that? Everybody in the office is curious. First Dan Mays submits his resignation without any notice. And now his wife has been transferred over to another division."

"It's the Grinch," Slam replied.

"The what?"

"The Grinch," Slam repeated. "The Grinch that stole Christmas. He's stashed it in a Coca-Cola warehouse somewhere, and we're trying to smoke it out. So far, all we've found is a couple of missing Easters and one lost Ground Hog Day. But we're getting close. Just yesterday Cramer caught the scent of eggnog emanating out of a warehouse in Spokane. Turned out to be a conventioneer from Waco, Texas, though, who'd gone out there last New Year's and had such a good time he didn't make it back home on time. Now he's afraid to go home; his wife, it seems, is a butcher. Wields a mean cleaver."

"Be serious, Slam."

"Okay. Look, all we're doing is taking a look to see how secure the computer system is. It's no big thing. Somebody should have done it long ago."

"How secure? How secure does it need to be? My gosh, Coca-Cola isn't the Defense Department, even though we may like to think we're more important than the government. Somebody is going to steal classified Coca-Cola information, like how many days vacation a Clerk III has accrued? That's ridiculous."

"Not really," Slam responded. The jocularity was gone. "Every record on that computer represents time, if nothing else. Lose them, through negligence or malice, and it would cost Coke a huge sum to compile them again. And that's assuming all of them could be reconstituted. Some of that data is stored only inside the computer."

"You're right, I'm sure," Laura said. "I just got the impression it was more than that. That perhaps something was wrong."

"I think your job's safe," Slam said teasingly. "That is, unless you've got a garage full of purloined Christmas presents. Is that a strand of tinsel I detect deep in your auburn tresses?"

"That, I'm sure, is one of the many strands of gray hair I have acquired since I began spending too much time with a harebrained immigrant from some unknown planet," Laura replied, laughing.

"The rink is right ahead. I'm going to warn you again. Pull any funny stuff out on the floor, and I'll cut you off at the knees. Roller-skating is not the best idea you've had. I prefer my wheels to come with an automatic transmission and velour seats."

"You have indeed shown admirable taste in that department," Slam said as he patted the Audi's upholstery. "But I still think we should have come on Themisticles."

"No way, Jose," Laura said firmly. "If I have to take a trip to the hospital emergency room, I'm not going to do it on the back of a motorcycle. That's final."

* * *

Will Posey looked downcast, like a kid who'd just found out his favorite Saturday morning cartoon had been canceled. He looked at Cramer almost as if he was pleading.

"Are you sure? Don Ball is one of our best people. He's been our division employee of the month twice. He's never taken a single sick day. We have to force him to take vacations. He goes to my church. Heck, my daughter's even gone out with him a couple of times when she's been home from college. We've got to know what we're talking about on this one."

"I don't think there's any doubt," Slam Duncan interjected quietly, but with a conviction Cramer found compelling. "Not taking vacations is a red flag of a fraudster. Working long hours and odd hours may be a red flag." Duncan gestured with his left hand, flashing the Ace bandage that he'd shown up wearing that morning. The computer whiz had mumbled something about a skating accident when Cramer had inquired. Duncan hadn't volunteered more, and Cramer hadn't pursued the matter because his associate was obviously a bit chagrined about the injury. Probably something to do with that attractive young woman Duncan had been squiring around, Cramer thought wryly. The course of young love obviously had a few unexpected and painful turns.

"We've tracked it back now for six months, and cross-referenced it to every operator who's worked here during that time," Duncan was continuing. "It's Ball, all right. Or at least part of the problem is. Here, let me show you."

With a start, Cramer realized he was relieved to let Duncan take the lead in the conference. Cramer was nothing if not perceptive. The esteem in which Ball was held by senior and junior staffers alike had not escaped him, and he had not looked forward to laying out the facts for Posey. But that was part of the job of an auditor, and he had long ago learned to distance himself from it.

No, this was something else. Where his profession was concerned, Cramer let no one in front of him unless the person had earned it. It came as a surprise to discover that the rambunctious, irreverent, outrageous Slam Duncan, over the past two weeks, had somehow sneaked up on the blind side of Cramer's respect. With a smile and a new perspective, he relaxed and for the first time really watched Duncan at work.

"Like I say, we went back six months," Duncan was saying. "We charted the shift of every operator you have in the division. Then we charted the time periods when we know, beyond any doubt, that you had lost computer time. We were able to verify that time had been lost by comparing the logs and repetitive programs that require essentially the same amount of time each time they are run. We found one operator who was on duty on each occasion that you lost computer time. The operator was Don Ball."

"Is there any other explanation?" Posey asked. The resignation in his voice was almost tangible.

No, Duncan replied. "I wish there was. But there isn't."

"Well, I guess that's that, then. Get it all lined up, and we'll have him in after lunch."

"There's one other thing," Duncan said. Cramer sat up expectantly. Duncan had not mentioned to him anything other than the same information he'd given Posey.

"He either doesn't care he's caught, or he wants to be identified. One of these times when there was unauthorized use was just last week, after he was aware we were conducting an audit."

"I'll have him in at 2 o'clock," Posey said. "I'll want both of you here when I confront him."

* * *

"Yes, sir," Ball said as he strode into Posey's office. "You wanted to see me?" The words were hardly uttered before the employee caught sight of Cramer and Duncan, seated on the sofa across from Posey's desk. Cramer watched closely. He saw no visible evidence that the presence of the two auditors caused Ball any consternation.

"Sit down, Don," Posey replied. "There's a problem we need to discuss with you. You've met Lenny Cramer and Mr. Duncan, I believe?" Cramer smiled inwardly: It was "Lenny Cramer," but "Mr. Duncan." Looks like the buttoned-down corporation mind-set has taken root with my old friend, he thought. He can't bring himself in a business conference to use a nickname like "Slam" or "Bo."

"Yes, I've been talking with both of them for about a week now," Ball responded. "What's the problem?" This time, Cramer noted, there was a hint of apprehension in the youngster's voice.

"It seems there has been some unauthorized use of the computer," Posey said sternly. "It has been traced to you, as late as last week. That's pretty serious, Don. It can mean termination. Want to tell me about it?"

Watching Ball's face was like watching a Christmas sparkler fade and die. The brightness ebbed, and nothing but the dry ash of despair remained. The long silence that ensued was broken only by the creak of the sofa as Duncan shifted his weight.

Finally, Ball straightened and said in a voice low but resolute. "You're right, Mr. Posey. I have been using the system, for about two years now. Not very much, never more than 10 minutes at a time. I'm sorry I did, and it was a stupid thing to do. But I did, and I'll own up to it whether you've got any evidence of it or not."

"How about telling us about it?"

"There's nothing much to tell." Ball was regaining control, and the confidence had returned to his voice.

I like this kid, Cramer thought. It's a shame he had to pull something like this. Let's hope he hasn't been up to some really dirty tricks.

"About two years ago, I purchased some software for a baseball card inventory and value system. That's what I've been doing..., updating my baseball card inventory. I only do it on my breaks. That's all."

"That's all! What do you mean, 'That's all?" Posey said with great agitation. "Don't you know that's a cardinal rule around here! Never bring in any outside programming? My goodness, son, surely you realize what could happen to our system if a virus ever got into it?"

"I know it's against company policy, Mr. Posey." Ball was contrite, but his demeanor was far from hangdog. He was pleading his case, and doing a pretty good job, Cramer thought. "But I want you to understand. My system at home is secure. Nothing has ever gone into it that didn't come still wrapped in cellophane from the manufacturer. I used brand-new disks to copy the software onto, and that's what I uploaded to our system. I know it doesn't mean anything to you, but I wouldn't even download anything from Coke's computer into mine. Once I worked out the inventory on our system, I went home and duplicated it on mine. I'm sure my system is free of any viruses. I'm not sure about the company's."

"I know you don't have a lot of background in computers. You may not understand that there's almost no way to detect the presence of a virus. Once it gets into a system some way—by being programmed in, or by having it downloaded from somewhere else,—you often can't detect it. I know what damage they can do. They can wipe out every bit of programming. They're malevolent, and anybody who'd infect a system with a virus has got to be sick. Anybody who would permit one to get into a system is inexcusably negligent. I know that. I may have been stupid in breaking a company rule, but our system hasn't been compromised because of me. I'll take my licks—I know I've got 'em coming—but you've got greater security problems to worry about."

"What do you mean?" Posey demanded. All three men were immediately alert, intent on what Ball was saying.

"Come on and I'll show you," Ball said, rising.

Just as Ball finished speaking, the phone rang. Posey answered and after a moment said, "Lenny, Slam, how about y'all go check this out. I need to handle this call." Don Ball led Cramer and Duncan to the information systems department.

Walking down the hall Cramer asked, "Aren't you a little too old to collect baseball cards?"

Ball's eyes lit up. "Baseball cards can be a lucrative investment."

"Baseball cards?" Cramer questioned in disbelief.

"Absolutely. A T206 Honus Wagner card from a 1909–11 set, with a crease, sold for $110,000 in 1988. Fewer than 100 of these cards are known to be in existence. In February 2007, a better one sold for $2.35 million, and again in September 2007, the same one sold for $2.8 million. Good profit. The Goudey Gum Company 240-card collection from 1933-including Babe Ruth and Lou Gehrig-sells for about $18,000."

Cramer said, "My mother threw away all of my baseball cards and comic books many years ago."

"That's probably why the old baseball cards are so valuable," Ball replied. "Did you have any DC *Detective Comics*? A complete mint run of *Detective Comics* retails for about $150,000. Over the past five year period the average yearly return has been 36%."

"Holy Bat Caves," Slam said mockingly. "I read Batman and Superman comics as a kid."

"Batman, about $47,000 and Superman, say $65,000," Ball stated. "Of course, it's hard to find high-quality investment comics. The acid left in comic book paper during the manufacturing process is the major cause of aging and yellowing."

"Why do you need a computer inventory?" asked Crammer.

"So many cards," answered Ball. "A complete *annual* set of every player who goes to spring training camps contains at least 750 cards, costing about $20."

Cramer laughed and said, "Next you'll tell me you sold short Pete Rose cards when they investigated him for gambling."

"Hey, don't laugh. There are even counterfeit Pete Rose cards. You could have sold short Wade Boggs or Steve Garvey. But let me tell you about the most infamous baseball card ever issued—the 1989 Fleer Bill Pipken card. Number 616."

Ball lowered his voice, "It's the Jesse James of baseball cards. Bill Pipken, a so-so second baseman, posed with an obscenity printed on the knob of his bat. After Fleer wiped the egg off their face, they recalled the pornographic card. It's worse than Claude Raymond posing with his uniform zipper open."

Chapter 7

The several types of statistical sampling plans used by auditors may be generally classified into two categories, attribute sampling plans and variables sampling plans. Attribute sampling is used to obtain a measure of the occurrence rate of a particular characteristic in a population. Variables sampling plans are used to estimate a value range for a characteristic in a population.

—J.W. Cook and G.M. Winkle

The information systems department was a couple of floors below Posey's office. When they arrived, Ball sat down at his computer workstation. The workstation was an IBM microcomputer hardwired to the Coke mainframe. In other words, Ball could run any number of applications at his microcomputer or tie into the mainframe for mainframe applications using his micro as a smart terminal.

Cramer noticed a book, *Standard Catalog of Baseball Cards*, on Ball's desk. He picked up and flipped through a softback book entitled *How to Collect Baseball Cards*.

Ball motioned for Cramer and Posey to take a seat. Ball swallowed hard and then said, "Heck, I didn't think updating my inventory occasionally would raise any eyebrows when the higher-ups were using the computer a hundred times more often for their unofficial jobs. Just look at this." At that, Ball's fingers began flying over the keyboard.

After logging in his user-ID, DBALL, and password, FIREBALL, Ball retrieved the mainframe's computer log and displayed it on his microcomputer's monitor screen. The log listed all the jobs run on the Coke mainframe computer for the past 30 days. He pointed to some line items here and there as he scrolled through the log. He said as he pointed, "You can see my inventory activities appear in the log as 'log time,' interruptions between processing of other programs. Of course you already know this. That's how you fingered me, isn't it?"

"Get to your point," Duncan said, getting rather bored looking at the computer log.

"Yes, get to your point," Cramer added, "You said you had something to show us." Cramer removed his photo-tinted grey glasses in order to see better.

"Well, before I do, I want to know what's in it for me. I don't like squealing on a fellow computer jock, but I just want you to know my game-playing is really insignificant compared to other people's unofficial use of the system."

"What makes you think you have something we don't already know?" Duncan replied sharply.

"Maybe I don't, but how are you going to know if I don't tell you?" Ball replied cautiously.

"Sure, if you have something really important, we won't make a big deal out of your baseball card inventory. Of course, you'll have to give us a couple of pieces of bubblegum. But don't push us, Don. Remember, you're the one in trouble," Cramer said with a frown.

"No bubblegum in sports cards anymore. All right, then, look at this," Ball pointed to the amber screen.

Cramer and Duncan looked. "I don't get it," Duncan said. "That's where somebody ran the online query and search program. What's so unusual or revealing about that?"

"Nothing, if that was the only time," replied Ball. "But look here and here." Ball pointed to a score of similar listings as he continued scrolling down the screen. "The key thing," Ball added as he scrolled and pointed, "is the user ID number. It's not on the registered ID list. It shouldn't work. This person shouldn't be able to do this. He didn't just come up with someone else's valid ID and associated password. He must have gotten in using a trap door. I haven't bothered to see when it started, but he's been doing this hacking for at least the past two years. That's when I first noticed it, anyway. I didn't turn him in because I thought it might be one of my buddies in operations. Later I found out it wasn't."

Duncan interjected, "Well, why didn't you at least bring it up then?"

"Why?" asked Ball, "I couldn't see any harm being done. Shoot, it might just be some kid out there hacking. I didn't want anyone to get in trouble over nothing. Besides, when I was in high school I used to hack and tried to break into every computer system I could—just for the fun of it. I never hurt anything. It was just a game with me, as well as some of my friends."

"My point is that our system," continued Ball, "has some real security problems. This illegal entry is just one example of what might be going on all over the system. This log only covers activities in the inventory section of the system, which is where I do most of my programming."

"And your baseball cards inventory," added Duncan in a monotone. His face offered no hint of a smile.

"Right," said Ball with a grimace.

"So what do y'all think?" continued Ball.

"We'll let you know," replied Cramer. "Slam, let's go up to my office and discuss this. Don, we'll get back to you tomorrow." At that, Cramer and Duncan got up and walked out the door, leaving Ball with a solemn look on his face.

"So what do you think?" Cramer asked Duncan as they entered Cramer's temporary workstation at the Coke office.

"Well, the baseball cards inventory is harmless enough, but I can hardly believe Don didn't inform the systems manager of this security problem. I'm going to check into it, but I have a feeling this problem is bigger than just some pimple-faced high school kid hacking. For one thing, a hacker would have been bored to death looking at inventory records long before two years were up."

"I get your point, Slam. What about this 'trap door' thing? As I understand, that's a technique programmers use to get around controls, but exactly how do they do it?"

"It's no big deal, Lenny. When a program is being written or changed, it's possible for a programmer to include some breaks—

that is, trap doors—in the program code making it possible to insert additional instructions and to provide intermediate output capability. It's a handy tool for programmers trying to debug a system. Unfortunately, this practice also makes it possible to insert unauthorized program procedures. These unauthorized procedures facilitate abuse."

Cramer looked puzzled and asked, "Give me an example."

Slam replied, "The best example of a trap door program is what is commonly referred to as a ZAP program. Programmers typically set up a utility ZAP program to modify other programs and data while bypassing controls. Don't get me wrong, a ZAP program can have legitimate uses. Most programmers wouldn't misuse a ZAP program, but the potential is there. The worst part is that the use of a ZAP program leaves few footprints. A 'Trojan Horse' program is another type of trap door. It involves hidden programming code within another program to provide unauthorized entry into a system. Someone appears to have used a 'Trojan Horse' in this case."

"So you think it was a Coke programmer who's been searching the files for who knows what," interrupted Cramer.

"Probably. On the other hand, it could be an outside hacker, although it would take someone knowledgeable about both programming and the Coke computer system to pull it off. Perhaps a former Coke employee," Duncan answered.

"Then it could be an inside job?" asked Cramer.

"Well, yes, but let's not jump to conclusions. I have a few things to check out before I point any fingers. No one is beyond suspicion, even Don Ball. This stunt could be something he's done in addition to his baseball card inventory."

"Wait a doggone minute, Slam. He's the one who told us about this, remember?"

"Hey, it's a possibility. Accountants have to be skeptical—all the time. Trust, but verify, as President Reagan said. Ball might figure we can't find out who the culprit is. Plus, it's a great smokescreen. We're not worried about his extracurricular activities keeping track of baseball cards anymore. Of course, you're right—he's not a likely possibility. My point is, you have to keep your eyes open and not rule anything out. Don't faint, but it could even be your old friend, Posey."

Cramer's mouth dropped open, but before he could speak Duncan slapped him on the back and said, "Just kidding."

"I'm glad. You just don't know what an honorable guy Will Posey really is!" responded Cramer, still taken aback at this lighthearted character assassination of his old friend and current employer.

"No offense, Len, but just remember 'power corrupts and absolute power corrupts absolutely. Another red flag of a fraudster is a trustworthy employee.'"

"I'll buy that as a general rule, but there are individuals in this world who hold honor above petty material gains," said Cramer, feeling a little hostile toward Duncan.

"Whoa, buddy, I can see I've touched a nerve. It's just something about the computer that tempts some people to assume they can get away with anything. They think just because they do it on the computer, nobody will be able to trace their clandestine activities back to them."

"And often that's a valid assumption because the audit trail gets lost in the computer system." Cramer said, beginning to feel better toward Duncan again. "As British clergyman Charles Caleb Colton said two centuries ago, 'there are some frauds so well conducted that it would be stupidity not to be deceived by them.'"

"Right, old chap. The problem with many computer systems is that the audit trail has not been carefully maintained. Shoot, lots of systems were designed with little or no input from accountants. It's no wonder there's so much computer crime. The average computer crime has been estimated to cost $167,713. Why, the average armed robbery is only $250, and the average street crime is $35. Almost two hundred grand is a pretty big temptation. What's more amazing is the chance of prosecution is almost nonexistent. Statistics show the bigger the dollar amount of a crime, the smaller its probability of prosecution."

"You must be kidding!"

"I wish I was. It certainly contradicts my idea of justice in America. Hey, we've been jabbering for quite a spell. My dinner alarm clock," said Duncan pointing to his abdomen, "is telling me it's time to go home and chow down."

"You're right. My daughter, Becc, is cooking up something special tonight. You want to join us?"

"Thanks. Amazingly, my busy single's calendar is open, and I'm gonna take you up on that offer."

"Great, you want to ride over with me?"

"Nah. I've my chopper in the parking lot. Can't leave that fine machine unattended after hours. I need to stop at a Starvin' Marvin and get some gas. I'll meet you at your bungalow in an hour—if that's OK?"

"Perfect. See you then," Cramer replied. Duncan stood and walked out of Cramer's office.

As he walked toward his office, Duncan thought that Cramer wasn't such a bad guy for an old professor. Of course, Cramer wasn't really that old; it was just that all professors seemed old. Then he laughed as he thought that was what he was going to be one day—an old professor—if he could ever get his dissertation written. He knew that half the people who start dissertations, never finish them. Well he wasn't going to be in that floundering boat—not after all the hours of coursework he had already invested in his quest for the doctorate degree—the union card to teach at a major university.

* * *

"Dad, how could you? You didn't bother to call and tell me we were having company for dinner? I've never made lasagna before! What if it's not any good?"

"You're right, Becc, I should have called to ask you if it was OK." Then Cramer sang, "Don't worry, be happy," recalling an old tune that had been playing on the radio lately.

Becc chuckled, "*Please*, Dad, no singing."

"Wait a minute, little girl, you didn't complain when you were a youngster."

"Well, maybe so, but would you put some *real* music on for our dinner guest? You're sure he's not a picky eater?"

Cramer walked from the kitchen and dining area into the living room where his antique armoire stood. He called to Becc, "In the mood for classical?"

"Sure, Dad, anything that goes with lasagna is fine."

The armoire had been converted into an entertainment center. A few years ago, Cramer had purchased the armoire at an antique auction and added the shelves later. He was quite pleased with the result. He enjoyed an occasional project that required working with his hands.

Cramer selected one of his favorite CDs, one featuring Mozart's five authenticated violin concertos. He then returned to the dining area to help with dinner preparations by setting the table. Becc was still preparing the meal in the adjoining kitchen area. "May I help?" he asked.

"No thanks, *Poppa*, your dinner is almost ready," Becc replied in her Italian accent. "I just hope our guest arrives soon. I'm taking the lasagna out of the oven, and it should sit for only about 10 minutes." Just then the doorbell rang.

Cramer walked over and opened the front door. "Greetings, Sir, please enter my humble abode."

"Why, thank you, my good man. Mmmmm, something smells great. Italian?"

"Indeed, follow me to the dining area and let me introduce you to the chef."

Cramer continued as they entered the dining area, "My daughter, Becc, is a promising Italian chef."

"Please, Dad, you're embarrassing me. Don't believe my dad until you taste the lasagna. It's my first try."

"Well, as I was saying, this is my daughter, Becc, a worried Italian chef. Becc, this fine gentleman is Slam Duncan, the computer whiz I was telling you about."

"I'm pleased to meet you, Mr. Duncan."

"Slam, please," Duncan interjected. "The pleasure is all mine. And dinner smells great."

"I hope you like lasagna." Becc said.

"I love anything Italian," Duncan responded.

"What would you like to drink, Mr. Duncan, I mean Slam?"

"Water, please."

"I'll take iced tea, Becc," added Cramer.

"Let's all go to the table then. We can start on our salad, and I can learn more about the mysterious world of auditing," Becc said with a grin.

As they sat down, Duncan tipped his head to emphasize he was listening. "Mozart, right?"

"Well, now, aren't you the cultured fellow. I knew you were an unusual character. At least a strange combination of computer jock and motorcyclist. I certainly didn't think you had time for the more refined aspects of western civilization." Cramer smiled as he picked up his salad fork.

"Becc, I hope your father has not told you anything about me. I would have thought that he, being an accounting professor, would know we accountants are not the dry little twerps that Hollywood makes us out to be."

Cramer and Becc both laughed. Duncan's almost six and a half foot frame was certainly not little, and his personality was far from dry. Becc responded, "All I really know is that you were recommended to Dad and Mr. Posey by an old college buddy named Howie. Dad says you know your stuff, and he's glad you're working with him."

Cramer interrupted with a mouthful of salad, "Now that's all true, except maybe the 'glad' part." Cramer broke into a big grin. He enjoyed kidding around with Duncan. He began to think of himself at Duncan's age, full of vim and vitality, ready to take on the world.

Of course, he was still ready to take on the world; although he had eased off a tad on the vim and vitality stuff. The last few years had been a rough experience, but Duncan was somehow having a rejuvenating effect on him. Funny, how at first, he didn't particularly like Slam's cavalier attitude, not to mention his black motorcycle. Oh, well, sometimes people are not what they first appear to be.

Becc interrupted his "wool gathering." "OK, guys, it's time to dip into the lasagna. Let me serve your portions. The pan is too hot to pass around the table."

"Thanks," said Duncan as he handed Becc his plate. Becc gave Slam a generous slice, and then took her father's plate and did the same. As they took their first bites, she asked, "Well? Well? Don't keep me in suspense!"

"Delicious," responded Duncan while chewing his first bite. "My compliments to the chef."

"Scrumptious, daughter," added Cramer.

"I'm so relieved," said Becc. "You can have all you want. I made a ton."

Later Duncan and Cramer had seconds, and Duncan thirds.

As Mozart's fifth violin concerto entered its finale, Duncan remarked, "Isn't that great. Can you believe he wrote that and his first four violin concertos before he was 20 years old?"

"Yes, he was a genius," stated Becc. "In fact, he wrote all five violin concertos in less than a year."

"Amazing," said Cramer.

"Mozart?" asked Becc.

"No. The way you two have these facts and figures in your heads. All I know is that I like the music."

"Oh, really, Dad. You know all sorts of trivia about Mozart, Beethoven, Bach, and lots of other classical composers."

"Well, I suppose it is true that Schroeder and I consider Ludwig van Beethoven the greatest musician who ever lived. The fact that he was a German composer and possibly a friend of my ancestors has nothing to do with my high regard for his music."

Amused, Duncan asked, "So, you know something about your roots, eh? Well, I'm a wee bit of a highlander myself. No great composers I know of, but there was a great poet from bonny Scotland by the name of Robert Burns."

"Scotland? Well, well, I knew there was something about you I liked," quipped Cramer.

"That's where another branch of our family came from, Slam," joined in Becc. "My great-great-great grandfather came to America in the 1830s. Dad has an old family Bible in which one of our ancestors recorded family events, births and marriages and such."

"Well, that's great," said Slam. "I wish I knew more about my family history; genealogy is fascinating to me. I've heard many stories about my family history, but unfortunately don't have much in writing, like birthdates and marriages. No one seemed to take the time to write down these things in my family. I do know that one ancestor came over in the late 1700s. One of my great-greats supported the attempt of Bonnie Prince Charlie to claim the throne of England. After which things didn't go so well for the Scots, and many left for the Land of Opportunity."

"I know about that from English Literature," added Becc. "He was Prince Charles Edward Stuart. Too bad for him and the Scots. The English brutally beat them at the Battle of Culloden Moor. Mid-1700s, I think?"

"You have English literature in the ninth grade?" asked Duncan.

"Actually it was an advanced literature class back at my junior high in Philadelphia. You learn so much about history from literature, and history is my favorite subject."

"Well, that's only because you haven't had any computer classes yet," Duncan said with a laugh.

"Actually, Slam I've been learning about computers since kindergarten," responded Becc. "Speaking of school, if you will excuse me, I need to get started on my homework. Can you believe it! School just started, and I have a report to write."

Cramer smiled. "That's fine, dear. I'll get the dishes later."

"I know you will, Dad. Remember our agreement. Just because you brought company home doesn't get you out of it. Good night, Slam. It was nice to meet you. Don't let Dad talk your ears off."

"Nice to meet you, Becc. Dinner was delicious. What's the agreement?"

Cramer joined in, "Whoever cooks doesn't have to clean up. Becc cooked, so I'm the kitchen crew."

Becc nodded, "Right. I'm glad you liked dinner, Slam. I hope you and Dad have a great audit together at Coke." With that Becc rose from the table and headed to her room.

"You have a great daughter, Len. It must be swell being a father. Although I know it's gotta be hard being a single parent."

"You're right on that one, Slam. I just hope I'm doing an adequate job. There have been some tough times since I lost my wife. Suppose we move into the living room where we can sit back in some easy chairs. Would you like a liquid refreshment? We have coke, tea, lemonade, or milk?"

"Lemonade, please."

As they rose from the table, Cramer said, "Go make yourself comfortable." He pointed toward the living room and then headed toward the refrigerator.

In a minute, Cramer entered the living room holding two tall glasses of ice-clinking lemonade. He said, "it's not a mansion, but it meets our needs."

"It looks a lot better than my bachelor pad. Ahh, this is a comfortable chair," remarked Duncan as he relaxed on the furniture.

"So where are you from besides Scotland, Slam?"

"I grew up in Wayne County, Mississippi. Believe it or not, the Scottish influence was very strong there. The Scots established the first school in the county in 1812. They didn't even speak English. They spoke Gaelic."

"I know a little about Gaelic. Eighteen letters in the alphabet, compared to English's twenty-six."

"That's right. One old Scotsman, Sir George MacKenzie, said, "our pronunciation is like ourselves, fiery, abrupt, sprightly, and bold.""

Cramer added, "The Scots were a tough, thrifty, hard-working people. They made good pioneers. They were fiercely independent, possessed a strong love of family and country, and had stern moral values."

"Hmmm, haven't changed much have they, Lenny?"

"No, I guess not. There's a movement in Scotland even now to separate from Great Britain. Apparently many of them feel they didn't get their fair share of the North Sea oil revenues."

"Are you serious? Could they really separate from Great Britain? The South tried to separate from the U.S. in the American Civil War. The results weren't too good."

Cramer answered, "It's a different situation in Britain. Scotland and England were separate countries for most of their history. They fought many a bloody battle with each other before joining together as the United Kingdom of Great Britain. The British flag, the Union Jack, is a combination of the old Scottish and English flags."

Cramer continued, "One issue of British pound notes features a picture of Robert the Bruce, the Scottish king who thoroughly whipped the English at the Battle of Bannockburn in the 1300s. I saw the battlefield during some free time while attending a conference at the

University of Stirling. It seems that the English executed one of Scotland's major heroes, William Wallace. As a result, the Scots were fired up by the time the English army made it to Bannockburn."

"I bet," laughed Duncan. "Of course the original Scots had already made a mark on history as fierce warriors."

"You mean the Picts," interjected Cramer. "The Romans may have conquered Europe, but the Roman emperor, Hadrian, had to build a wall to protect Roman Britain from the northern tribes."

"Besides being tough soldiers, the Scots are renowned as engineers," added Duncan.

"Precisely why the Starship Enterprise's chief engineer was Montgomery Scot," said Cramer recalling his favorite TV reruns.

"So you're a Trekkie?" asked Duncan.

"I like science fiction and roller coasters," replied Cramer.

"Strange combination. Not too many years ago, computers were science fiction," said Duncan. "The first computers were used in business in the late 1950s."

"It's sure easier writing a dissertation with the use of a computer and word-processing. I typed mine on a typewriter. That makes me feel like a dinosaur!" Cramer smiled. "By the way, how is your dissertation coming along?"

"Slow, despite the aid of the computer. A doctoral program is somewhat like a fraternity initiation, except mental hazing seems to be permitted." Slam half joked. "Some people told me I shouldn't be taking time out to do anything else, like this consulting job. But, hey, I gotta eat."

"I'm glad you did, Slam. I really need your help on this Coke job. What do you think we should tell Don Ball tomorrow? Whatever we decide, I'll discuss with Will."

"Personally, I don't have a problem with his baseball card program. He seemed to be doing his job. Instead of a coffee break, he simply took a baseball card break. On the other hand, he should not have loaded the program into the Coke system. That should be a strict no-no. He could have kept the program on a disk and used it on his microcomputer. The worst thing he did in my judgment is not informing his superior about the apparent break-in by the person with the unlisted ID. For now, why don't you just tell Ball that he's officially reprimanded and not to use the computer for unofficial business any more?"

"Sounds reasonable. I'll discuss it with Will in the morning. It appears Coke needs more specific written policies on controls and security. As far I can tell, Ball didn't break any written rules."

"Good documentation of controls is essential to an efficient accounting information system," added Slam. "The programs, control procedures, run manuals, and the likes need to be well documented and kept up-to-date."

"What do you think about this apparent hacker? Did he get in through a trap door? And if so, is he a Coke employee or an outsider?"

"Lenny, I have a suspicion, and once I check it out, I'll get back to you. There are a number of people who could do it, but why is still the big question. If the hacker limited himself to Ball's department, all he's looking at are inventory records."

"Could he have sent himself some supplies and then resold them?" asked Cramer. "He could have a shell corporation."

"I don't think so. Coke has a good separation of duties between record keeping and physical custody of assets. Shipping would have to approve that type of transaction, and the hacker wouldn't have the necessary authorization to get that approval. So, I don't think that would work."

Duncan continued, "Uh, oh," as he noticed the clock on the wall. "I'm afraid I've taken advantage of your hospitality. It's time for me to be moseying on home. I have had a great time. Nothing like a home-cooked meal, a much-needed break from bacheloring."

"Well, now, don't rush off, Slam. I've thoroughly enjoyed our conversation."

Duncan eased himself up from his chair after setting his empty glass on a side table. "No, I've gotta go get my beauty sleep. Thanks a heap for everything. I'll holler at you first thing in the morning."

Cramer rose and followed Duncan to the door. "I'm really glad I met Becc. Be sure to tell her again how much I enjoyed the lasagna."

"I'm glad you came over, and Becc really enjoyed meeting you, too."

"Good night," Duncan said as he opened the door.

"Good night, easy-rider," quipped Cramer as he watched Duncan walk toward the motorcycle parked in his driveway. "An interesting character, that Slam," thought Cramer as he closed the door. "This audit might be more fun than I first thought." Cramer picked up the two empty lemonade glasses and headed into the dining room. After clearing the table, he started for Becc's room to tell her good night, but the phone rang before he left the kitchen.

"Hello," he answered, wondering who would call this late.

"What? How? I can hardly believe it, Will. Yes, I'll come by early tomorrow." Cramer hung up the phone and thought his little operational audit was becoming rather complicated. The Coke computer system had come down with a pesky virus. "Tomorrow is going to be a tough day," he thought. He went by Becc's room. She was doing her homework while listening to music on her iPod. He told her good night. Later, in his room, he took a long time falling asleep. He kept thinking that he was overlooking something important.

Chapter 8

Many executives seem to be infatuated with the limit-
less information potential of computers—sometimes
at the real expense of the human thinking that ought
to be at the base of any analysis. When playing the en-
ticing "what if" games that computers make available,
beware of contracting "spreadsheetitis." And remember, machines cannot think (not yet); they can only re-
arrange what was furnished them previously.

—Philip Kropatkin

Cramer was always amazed by the impeccable neatness of Posey's
office. The desk was always organized. Only a few papers lay on
the desktop; apparently they related to the crisis at hand. Next to
the main desk was a smaller desk. On it was a Dell computer, a
color monitor, and an HP printer. Cramer then noticed the pho-
tograph on Posey's desk. It was a family picture of Will, his wife,
and two daughters. Momentarily, Cramer's heart ached for his wife.
He supposed that he would never really get over missing her. Amazing, how fast the memories returned.

"Will, you look like death warmed over. Didn't you sleep well?"
Lenny Cramer asked.

"Ha. Sleep? I wish. Computer people from the main office had
me up here most of the night. We've been trying to get the system
back up. As I told you last night, everything went down. Looks like
we may have lost some files."

"Let's start at the beginning, Will. What happened to the computer system? What caused it to go down?"

"It was a virus. The night operator indicated that there was a problem about six yesterday evening. By 7:30, things were getting out of control, so he called the systems manager at home. She came up here soon afterwards. She then called in the analysts from our main office about 10 o'clock. I called you soon after that. The virus crashed my subsystem." Posey waved his right arm. "That is, overseas development crashed first. Next, the inventory database went down. A couple of other systems were slightly affected before we got things under control."

Lenny knew firsthand what a virus could do. Virus programs instruct the host computer to summon stored files. When it does so, the virus program copies itself onto the files. Consequently, the computer's memory degenerates into a big mess. Hackers sometimes create viruses to show off their computer skills.

"Do you know the source of the virus?" asked Cramer.

"Not yet, but you need to talk to the systems manager for the details."

Just then Posey's phone rang. He answered, "Send him in." In a moment Duncan opened the door.

Before Cramer or Posey could speak, Duncan spoke in a rough imitation of John Wayne. "Well pilgrims, we'd best circle the wagons. We're under attack."

Posey tried to smile and said, "I'd laugh if I could."

"Slam, I'm afraid our employer hasn't had enough rest. I guess you've gotten the scoop."

"Just that a nasty bug seems to have infected our modern technology. Lucky for Coke they already have on hand two of the world's leading computer consultants."

"Where...." began Cramer before realizing Duncan was referring to the two of them. "Well, I wish I had so much self-confidence, Slam. This audit is turning into a little bigger problem than I've had to deal with before."

Cramer continued as he looked at Slam, "We need to go talk to the systems manager and find out exactly what happened." Cramer turned back to Posey and said, "Last night Slam and I discussed our smaller problem of Don Ball. He seems like a pretty decent fellow. We recommend you send him a reprimand letter with a warning not to update his baseball cards inventory or other games on company time. Additionally, you should send a memo to all appropriate personnel not to run unauthorized programs on Coke computers."

"Fine, I will. In the meantime, you computer whizzes can go give my computer a shot of something and get my system back up."

Cramer and Duncan both left Posey's office. They arranged an appointment with the systems manager later that morning. After the meeting with the systems manager, Cramer and Duncan went to Cramer's work area in the Coke building to discuss the meeting.

"So what do you think, Lenny? Does the systems manager really have everything under control?"

"He seems competent enough to me. I do appreciate his attitude toward hackers who load viruses into computer systems."

"Lock them up and throw away the key!" Duncan laughed. "You remember the big virus incident in November 1988?"

"Oh, sure, the Cornell graduate student who managed to shut down 6,000 computers around the country. The computers were connected through ARPAnet and other E-mail networks in the Internet loop. Some of the nation's top science and research centers were affected. That incident surely made a lot of people start thinking about computer security."

Cramer continued, "The worst part is that the guy became a hero to several thousand computer jocks. You know the type I mean. The ones who see security measures as challenges to overcome. A lot of press coverage focused on admiration of the guy's handiwork, but not his ethics. Some people tried to downplay the seriousness of what he did by explaining that his program was not a virus that destroys data, but a worm that simply uses up storage space. Whatever you want to call it, the bug stopped computer operations at centers all around the country. The creator of a virus can't be sure that it won't get out of control and destroy important data somewhere in a computer network."

"I couldn't agree more." Duncan broke into the lecture. "Whether it's a virus program or a worm program, it's a major headache for system users. Admittedly though, a virus that destroys irreplaceable data is much worse than a worm that simply brings the system to a halt."

Cramer nodded. "Looks like the Coke system was affected by a virus. But at least there was a backup for most of the data files that were destroyed."

"This type of incident is alarming to the external auditors. No doubt they'll be concerned about the system's internal controls when they discover that this occurred."

"Good point, Slam. I'm lecturing on the auditor's responsibility for internal control tomorrow in my auditing class."

Cramer glanced at the Dell personal computer on his desk and said, "Let's see if we can link to the mainframe system. The systems manager said it would be up and running by now."

Cramer logged onto the computer. "What the …" Cramer gasped. The screen displayed the following message:

LENNY CRAMER, QUIT THE AUDIT OR
YOUR NEXT LECTURE WILL BE YOUR LAST!!

Duncan's brow knotted as his eyes focused on Cramer's monitor screen. "Someone's gotta lot of nerve," Duncan flatly stated. "Either someone has a warped sense of humor, or this audit is becoming rather serious. Looks like we've scared someone."

"Apparently so," said Cramer in a slightly shaky voice. His throat was dry and his pulse was racing. He wanted to appear more at ease than he felt. "I don't like being threatened," he said with bravado.

Cramer continued speaking. "Professors don't usually have to deal with this sort of problem. I think I'll review all the workpapers, and see if I've overlooked something. I'm sure as heck not going to resign from the audit. What really puzzles me is what have we done to upset someone so much? We haven't found anything really bad. I guess we must be close to something, though."

"That's a good idea, Len. Take a second look at everything we've done so far. Do you think we should inform the local authorities about this threat?"

"No, I don't want to do that. I'd have to withdraw from the engagement then. Remember, I'm just starting up in Atlanta. I need the money. Coke wouldn't want the publicity. Let's just keep this message between the two of us. At least for now. Agreed?"

"Gosh, old buddy, are you sure? This threat seems to have me more worried than you."

Cramer was feeling more comfortable again. His pulse had slowed back to normal. "I'm sure, Slam. I doubt whoever made this anonymous threat has any intention to carry it out. Most people who threaten are just bluffing. So, do you agree to keep it confidential?"

"You're the boss. I need the money, too. I just hope we're doing the right thing."

With that Duncan walked to the door. Cramer followed him. "I'll see you tomorrow, Slam."

"OK. I'm going to do some more examination of the password security system. I think I'm close to figuring out who's been doing the unauthorized searches in the inventory system. After your threat, I'm more anxious than ever to know. They could be related."

"We'll see," said Cramer. At that Cramer returned to his desk. As he did so, Duncan watched with concern. He wondered if silence was the right thing? Should the cops be called? Well, he had given his word. He wouldn't tell anyone without informing Lenny first. He stopped fretting and walked away from Cramer's office. He headed toward his work center. When he arrived, he logged onto his computer.

"Well, well," he said to himself. "I'm glad I wasn't left out." The screen bore the message:

BEAUREGARD DUNCAN,
QUIT THE AUDIT WHILE YOU CAN
OR YOUR NEXT COMPUTER LOG ON
WILL BE YOUR LAST!!

A grim expression came over his face. "This audit is getting a little too personal. I won't put up with harassment," he thought angrily. He settled back in his chair and noticed his clenched fists. He laughed slowly.

Those fighting instincts were still there. No matter how civilized a person was, just underneath the surface was the deadliest animal on planet Earth. The human brain had made man the dominant species, and Duncan knew he would have to use his if he was to find the person behind this threat. As adrenalin pumped through his biosystem, he actually felt invigorated by this personal challenge from some anonymous person.

As with Cramer's message, Duncan knew there was no way to trace it. Both messages were too personal to be random messages. The culprit knew that Cramer was a professor, and that Duncan was something of a computer jock. Since he couldn't get any fingerprints from the message, he cleared the screen and went to work. Hours passed.

* * *

After the anonymous warning to quit the audit, Cramer worked the rest of the day trying to deduce who sent it. He thought much about the matter as he drove slowly up Martin Luther King's Freeway in the Atlanta evening rush hour traffic. Based on the work paper review, no one seemed to be seriously threatened by his forensic audit. Maybe that was the answer. The threat wasn't in the workpapers. As Slam had indicated, perhaps it was tied to the unauthorized searches in the inventory system by the presumed hacker. The hacker also was suspected of the virus incident.

Cramer continued thinking of the day's events. After the initial shock, the threat really didn't worry Cramer all that much. He had seen too much of life to be bothered greatly. He had faced other difficult circumstances, particularly the loss of his wife. He recalled his wild experience in Burma last year, and a Bible verse came into his mind. "Those who hope in the Lord will renew their strength. They will soar on wings like eagles; they will run and not grow weary, they will walk and not be faint."

He pulled into the driveway, turned off the ignition, and walked to the door. As he unlocked and opened the door, he didn't hear Becc. "Becc," he called. No answer. "Lord, protect us," he thought as he walked faster than usual to her bedroom. He looked in the doorway.

She looked up, iPod headphones on her head. "Hi, Dad," she said cheerily. "How was your day?" she asked, removing the headphones.

"Fine," he answered, breathing more easily. "Let's go get burgers for dinner. OK?"

"I would rather have chicken. Are you feeling well?"

"Yes, the traffic was rougher than usual." He fibbed. "I'm going to change. Then we'll go get burgers and chicken." He turned away from her doorway and walked to his room. He thought, "I'll be glad when this audit is over!" Today he disagreed with what Elvis Presley once said: "I have no use for bodyguards, but I have very specific use for two highly trained CPAs."

* * *

The J. Mack Robinson College of Business is located at 35 Broad Street on the corner of Marietta Street and Broad Street. The accounting department is located on the fifth floor, but classes are taught in other buildings. The business school is named after an entrepreneur, talented businessman, philanthropist, and breeder of thoroughbred racehorses. His endowment was $10 million. He owns approximately 90 horses and his farm has a 5/8 mile racetrack.

This fifth largest business school in the U.S is located in the heart of Atlanta, just minutes away from Coca-Cola, Turner Broadcasting, Bell South, Georgia Pacific, UPS, and Home Depot. Georgia State has around 28,000 students at the urban research university with no football team. The football era will begin in 2010.

"Margaret Barbera was very good with numbers. She could take a balance sheet, a set of account books, invoices, bills, and more, juggle and manipulate the figures and, presto, thousands became millions, losses became profits, profits became losses, sales soared or fell, whatever her employer desired, and it would take an expert auditor knowing precisely where to look and what to look for to figure out what she'd done, and even then, it still might slip by." Professor Cramer was in front of his auditing class quoting a passage from *The CBS Murders*, by Richard Hammer.

He liked to start off each of his auditing classes with something provocative from real life. The twenty-six older students were sitting in small, timeworn chairs in a room with pale white paint peeling from the walls. A couple of students were reading copies of *The Signal*, the weekly student newspaper.

Cramer continued the passage. "There is an underground of people like Margaret Barbera, eagerly sought after by businessmen in trouble, especially in volatile and unstable industries, such as garments and jewelry. Ask the right questions of the right people, and pretty soon a Margaret Barbera, or somebody much like her, will come knocking at the door."

As he tossed the softback novel back into his briefcase, he glanced out of the window. He saw street people strolling by outside. The auditing class had started at 5:30 in the general classroom building on the Georgia State University campus. He thought, "The word campus may not be the best description of Georgia State. Combat zone, maybe." Being on the semester system, this auditing class met twice a week, an hour and a half per class. Cramer was a subway stop professor—a part-time professor. Regrettably, universities and colleges were hiring more and more part-time professors.

"When you leave my course, I wish you to remember two words—trusted employee. They are the people who often commit fraud in many organizations." Cramer picked up a newspaper article and held it over his head.

"Last week's newspapers reported an accounting clerk allegedly stole as much as $6 million from a Houston custom window builder. She merely deposited checks meant for the business into her own bank account and spent millions. She had 100 rings, 61 pairs of designer sunglasses, 12 pairs of $2,000 shoes, and paintings and sculptures from Europe. She traveled extensively."

"A company spokesman's said she was trusted with the company's finances. 'She came up with us.' The cash flow problem she caused led to 30 lay-offs this year. You must be skeptical of all employees, especially trusted employees."

He put down the newspaper article and walked over to place his first sheet onto the Elmo projector. He chuckled softly. The glass top was dusty, so he leaned over and blew the dust from the surface of the projector. He still did not use PowerPoint slides in the classroom like most professors today. He preferred the older overhead projector, but the newer Elmo projector would do fine. Cramer pressed a button to turn on the Elmo to show his material on the classroom screen.

"Wisdom is knowing what to do; virtue is doing it," Cramer said. "Just saying you believe something isn't enough. You have to take action to prove those beliefs are valid. You've all heard the expression that talk is cheap. Anyone can learn how to talk the talk, but it takes dedication to walk the walk. Today we're going to discuss a crucial element of the auditing profession, of any profession, and that crucial element is ethics."

Cramer continued. "Individual responsibility is the critical issue in establishing a code of conduct. A code of professional conduct is formulated to provide a minimum level of conduct for the well-being of a profession. The American Institute of CPA's Code of Professional Conduct describes the responsibility of the CPA to colleagues, clients, and the general public."

A student wearing a t-shirt with the blue Pounce, the university's panther mascot, on it raised his hand, and Cramer responded. "Yes, you have a question, Ralph?"

"Not a question, exactly, Dr. Cramer. But it seems to me that it's a waste of time talking about ethics. Everyone knows you can't teach ethics and morality. Everyone's already made up their minds about those things before they get to college."

"Perhaps," said Cramer. "Supposedly college students still have an open mind. But whether your personal code of ethics parallels the Institute's is irrelevant. Either you follow the profession's code, or you get expelled from the AICPA."

Cramer added, "In fact, one reason we have a professional code of conduct is to provide some uniformity in the way different CPAs respond to similar situations. There are four distinct parts of the AICPA's Code: Principles of Professional Conduct, Rules of Conduct, Interpretations of Rules of Conduct, and Ethics Rulings."

Cramer gestured toward the screen. His sheet listed the six principles of professional conduct:

1. *Responsibilities.* In carrying out their responsibilities as professionals, members should exercise sensitive professional and moral judgments in all their activities.
2. *The Public Interest.* Members should accept the obligation to act in a way that will serve the public interest, honor the public trust, and demonstrate commitment to professionalism.

3. *Integrity.* To maintain and broaden public confidence, members should perform all professional responsibilities with the highest sense of integrity.

4. *Objectivity and Independence.* A member should maintain objectivity and be free of conflicts of interest in discharging professional responsibilities. A member in public practice should be independent in fact and appearance when providing auditing and other attestation services.

5. *Due Care.* A member should observe the profession's technical and ethical standards, strive continually to improve competence and the quality of services, and discharge professional responsibility to the best of the member's ability.

6. *Scope and Nature of Services.* A member in public practice should observe the Principles of the Code of Professional Conduct in determining the scope and nature of services to be provided.

Cramer pointed to the screen and continued his discourse. "These principles should be the basis of everything a CPA does. These basic principles were carefully evaluated by the Institute when the other three parts of the Code were established. Also, when a CPA encounters a situation in which there is no specific Rule of Conduct, Interpretation, or Ethics Ruling, then the CPA must be guided by these principles."

Cramer paused. "The Rules of Conduct provide the minimum levels of acceptable conduct. They are enforced by the Ethics Division of the AICPA. The Interpretations and Ethics Rulings provide more detailed guidance."

Another student raised a hand. "Yes," Cramer responded.

"I understand these are guidelines, but what actually happens to a CPA who breaks a rule?" An older student asked.

"It depends on the specifics of each individual case," Cramer replied. He then pulled out an old issue of *The CPA Letter* that contained the Semiannual Report of Joint Ethics Enforcement Program Activity. As he glanced at the dog-eared document, he said, "For example, in the last six months of 2008, the Ethics Committee disposed of 239 case investigations. Of those 239, 143 resulted in no violation findings, 31 in minor violation letters, and 26 in administrative reprimands. The remaining 29 investigations were either being prepared for or were submitted to the Trial Board."

A student interrupted. "What did the Trial Board do?"

Cramer frowned at the interruption. He was a stickler for students raising their hands. He continued with a frown at the student. "Well, during that same six-month period, the Trial Board expelled seven and suspended two members under automatic provision of bylaws. For example, being sentenced to a year or more in jail results in automatic expulsion. At Trial Board hearings, two members were suspended and required to take some CPE—uh, continuing professional education. Three members were admonished and required to take some CPE."

Cramer put on another sheet. "These are the Rules of Conduct." The screen showed Rules 101 to 505.

> INDEPENDENCE, INTEGRITY, AND OBJECTIVITY
> 101 Independence
> 102 Integrity and Objectivity
>
> COMPETENCE AND TECHNICAL STANDARDS
> 201 General Standards
> 202 Compliance with Standards
> 203 Accounting Principles
>
> RESPONSIBILITY TO CLIENTS
> 301 Confidential Client Information
> 302 Contingent Fees
>
> OTHER RESPONSIBILITIES AND PRACTICES
> 501 Acts Discreditable
> 502 Advertising and Other Forms of Solicitation
> 503 Commissions and Referral Fees
> 505 Form of Organization and Name

A student raised her hand. "Yes, Beth," he acknowledged along with a nod of his head.

"What happened to the 400s?" she asked.

"Good question. The 400 series related to encroaching on the practice of colleagues. Those rules were determined to be in restraint of trade by the courts and have been suspended at this time."

"An area closely related to ethics is what should the auditors do if they become aware of an illegal act committed by a client firm's personnel. Guidance for the auditor's action is found in SAS No. 54, *Illegal Acts by Clients*, and SAS No. 53, *The Auditor's Responsibility to Detect and Report Errors or Irregularities*. Is the auditor expected to find illegal acts?"

When no one raised his hand, Cramer called on the first student who made eye contact. "Joyce?"

"Well, Dr. Cramer, I'm not sure, but it seems to me that they would only be expected to find the illegal act if it had a material effect on the financial statements."

"Excellent, Joyce. You are absolutely correct according to the AICPA. But SAS No. 99 has expanded the fact-finding phase beyond the normal audit. We will cover SAS No. 99 later this semester. Auditors must now assess a company's programs and controls that deal with identifying fraud risks. Brainstorming sessions, inquiry procedures, expanded analytical procedures, and more skepticism are now required of an auditor. Always remember that not finding the fraud will not advance you within your company."

Consider this scenario. You're auditing a computer manufacturer, and you're sampling the sales invoices and discover sales of computers with the latest technology to Vladimir Rocket Company in Tripoli, Libya. Is there a problem?"

Joyce raised her hand.

"Yes, Joyce," Cramer responded.

"I don't know this for sure, but I suspect we're not supposed to conduct business with countries like Libya. You know—terrorist city." The other students laughed.

"Good point. The CPA should make inquiries of the client's management concerning compliance with laws and regulations and preventive measures used by the client to prevent illegal acts. In addition to inquiries, there are other audit procedures that may detect illegal acts. For example, an illegal act may be discovered during compliance tests used to assess control risk, related tests of transactions and balances, and inquiries of the client's legal counsel. The illegal act may be the selling of technology to banned countries or as mundane as fraud by one of the client's personnel. Back to the question, what should you do as the auditor?"

"Call the cops," someone yelled. The class roared with laughter.

Cramer smiled. "Not exactly." Cramer read from the textbook, *Auditing Concepts, Standards, and Procedures.* "I'm reading from our textbook, Chapter 17. When the auditor's examination provides evidence that illegal acts may have occurred, the auditor should: (1) consider the implications of the act and its effect on the statements, (2) consult with the client's legal counsel, (3) report the incident to a sufficiently high level of management and the client's audit committee, and (4) consider performing additional auditing procedures, if practical or possible."

"A disclaimer of opinion is generally issued by the auditor if a CPA is unable to obtain sufficient competent evidence regarding a possible illegal act. However, if the auditor concludes that an illegal act has occurred that is material and believes disclosure should be made in the statements, a qualified or adverse opinion should be expressed if disclosure is not made. A qualified opinion or disclaimer should be expressed if the auditor is unable to reasonably estimate the effect the illegal act has on the statements."

"Even if an illegal act is not considered material by a CPA, the auditor should request that management take appropriate remedial action. If management refuses to do so, the auditor should consider withdrawing from the present engagement and possibly severing any future relationship with the client. It is the duty of management, not the auditor, to notify outside parties of illegal acts committed by the client. End of quote."

Cramer discussed a few more cases before dismissing class. After class Cramer thought about his upcoming trip to Washington. He had been requested to appear in a few weeks at a Congressional hearing concerning the integrity of the accounting profession. Cramer sincerely hoped the profession would indeed abode by a high code of ethics.

Cramer left the classroom building. He felt a grumpy mood coming over him as he walked to his car. "I'm going to cheer myself up before I get home and see Becc," he thought as he got on his car to drive home.

When he arrived home, he found Becc watching a Star Trek episode on a DVD. "Which do you like the best, the original shows or Star Trek: Next Generation?" he asked as he walked into the living room. Cramer always enjoyed discussing the merits of the various characters among the two closely related TV series. He was inwardly pleased that Becc had become a major fan of the crews of both captains, Kirk and Picard.

"Gee, Dad, that's hard to determine. Last time we talked about this I picked Next Generation, but lately I've been watching your DVDs of the original series. I really like that episode called "City on the Edge of Forever.'"

"Oh, yeah, that's my favorite episode! McCoy goes through a time portal called the 'Guardian of Forever' and accidentally changes history. Kirk and Spock go after him. They wind up on Earth during the 1930s. Kirk falls in love with a character played by Jane Seymour."

"That's it. Do you remember that hysterical scene where Kirk explains to the police officer how Spick's ears became pointed?"

Cramer and Becc both grinned.

Becc's grin faded abruptly. She said, "There were a lot of humorous moments on that episode, but the ending was so sad! Why, I almost cried."

"The ending was very solemn, but all Trekkies know that it's James T. Kirk's love for his ship, the Enterprise, that keeps him going during moments of despair."

Father and daughter talked for another couple of minutes about Star Trek before calling it a night. Cramer wasn't looking forward to the next day. Tomorrow morning, he was scheduled to appear in court as an accounting expert witness. He felt restless, but strangely fell asleep almost the instant his head hit the pillow.

Chapter 9

Taking a job with a nationally recognized public accounting firm has provided many fast trackers with a solid career foundation. It offers the experience needed to sit for the CPA exam and provides an overview and technical expertise not always available at a smaller practice.

—Arielle Emmett

Cramer woke early. He was anxious about his court battle, which was scheduled first thing this morning. Almost 90 percent of disputes are settled before trial. Most cases are won and lost on disposition. The attorneys review the dispositions to evaluate the dispute for settlement or trial. Thus, both he and his opposing expert must have done a good job.

Even though he had served as an expert witness on other occasions, there were always some butterflies before appearing in court. "Last minute jitters," he thought. "Some people claim a little nervousness helps you do a better job."

Cramer had a light breakfast with Becc. She said goodbye and left for school, leaving Cramer alone to ponder his court case. He decided to take a cab. He needed to look over his notes and focus on the dispute at hand, instead of fighting traffic. His attorney's client was a CPA firm that was being sued by a group of disgruntled ex-stockholders—called plaintiffs. They were ex-stockholders because their former investment had gone belly-up. They contended that the CPA firm—the defendants—had failed to perform the audit properly. Cramer called a local cab company, and in a few minutes he was riding into downtown.

"Everyone wants to sue the CPA firm," thought Cramer as he rode along unconcerned with the traffic problems confronting the cabbie. "They are deep pockets."

Cramer began to ponder the litigation problem of American society. "The lawsuit problem had gotten worse in recent years. The underlying context of a lawsuit against accountants is often a client firm's financial disaster. An external user of the audited financial statements—a creditor or investor—has lost money. The only suffering on the part of the accountant is possibly an unpaid bill. Thus, they are the only ones who have not financially suffered from the disaster. They also are still solvent, and are often perceived as having 'deep pockets.' As a result, they are obvious lawsuit targets, because if one does win a judgment against the accountants, the judgment is collectible. Civil damage suits against professionals were rare until the mid-1960s. At that time an outbreak of civil malpractice suits were aimed first at physicians, then at accountants, and lawyers."

"Today's dispute was a civil trial, not a criminal trial. He would be testifying for the CPA firm—the defendant. But he had to remain nonbiased. An expert witness is an advocate for the truth."

Cramer slowly shook his head as he continued pondering the problem. "Much of the legal liability crisis is due to a tort system which may be out of control. Innocent victims of negligence should, of course, be fairly compensated for economic damages, but society cannot afford the costs of protecting everyone from his or her own folly."

He remembered a case in which a youth was paralyzed when he fell through a roof while burglarizing a school. The financial award he received was largely due to school officials having several prior warnings of the roof's dangerous condition. This particular incident seemed to indicate a need to return common sense to the law. "Should someone willfully doing wrong, in this case burglarizing, be given an award?" Cramer thought not.

Cramer was so lost in thought that the cab ride seemed to take no time. After paying the cabbie and pocketing the receipt, he walked quickly up the courthouse steps. Following a brief greeting from his attorney outside the courtroom, he was soon on the witness stand, where he forcefully said "I will" when he was asked if he would tell the truth. He was able to turn the chair so he could speak to the jurors, rather than the questioning lawyers.

"Professor Cramer, for the court's record, please state your full name, spell your last name, and give your current address for our court reporter," spoke his retaining lawyer.

"Paul Leonard Cramer, the third, C-R-A-M-E-R, 1601 Elizabeth Avenue, Atlanta, Georgia."

"Dr. Cramer, we wish to thank you for testifying today as an expert witness about certain accounting matters. First, I have several questions for you concerning your background. Where did you obtain your Ph.D. degree?"

"University of Illinois."

"Where did you receive your MBA degree?"

"Harvard University."

"Where did you receive your bachelor's degree?"

"University of Massachusetts at Amherst."

Lenny had rehearsed most of these questions and answers before. Lenny liked the grueling task of preparing beforehand and participating in a courtroom battle over accounting principles. There was the challenge to react and respond to the many trick questions asked by the opposing attorney. Probably the stress was not worth the daily fees he received, but he loved it. He sometimes imagined the opposing attorney to be an aggressive college wrestler anxious to pin him to the rubber mat. Not one of those actors-wrestlers you see on television late at night on professional wrestling. Lenny always pinned his vicious opponent in his daydreams.

"Professor Cramer, have you written any accounting books?"

"I have written four accounting books. One principles of accounting textbook, a forensic accounting book, an auditing handbook, plus an accounting casebook for MBA students."

"Would you please explain what is meant by forensic accounting?"

"Briefly, forensic accounting is a science that deals with the relation and application of accounting facts to business and social problems." Cramer smiled and turned toward the jury. "As I tell my students, a forensic accountant is like a character on CSI Miami, except he uses accounting records and facts to uncover fraud, missing assets, insider tradings, and other white-collar crimes." Lenny turned back to the pinstriped lawyer.

"Dr. Cramer, where are you currently employed?"

"Georgia State University, and I have a private practice."

"Are you a Certified Public Accountant?"

"Yes, in Pennsylvania, since 1978," Lenny responded.

"Do you have any other professional certification?"

"Yes. CrFA. CFFA. CFF. FCPA."

"What do these symbols stand for, please?"

"CrFA means Certified Forensic Accountant. CFFA is a Certified Financial Forensic Analyst. CFF refers to Certified in Financial Forensics. FCPA is a Forensic CPA."

"Do you serve on the Board of Directors of any major corporations?"

"Yes, I serve on the Board of Directors of two of the top Fortune one hundred companies and for three smaller companies."

"Dr. Cramer, are you an outside consultant?"

"Yes, I have my own forensic accounting firm here in Atlanta."

"Please estimate how many professional articles you have written."

"About 75." Lenny shifted in the wooden chair.

"Are you on the editorial board of the *Journal of Forensic Accounting?*"

"Yes, I am," Cramer continued to look at the jurors as he spoke.

"Uh." The attorney shuffled several pages and then continued, "Have you ever appeared as an expert witness in the courtroom?"

"Yes. I have been an expert witness for accounting matters on about twelve different occasions—three oil companies, two banks, one insurance company, a manufacturing company, an accounting firm, the Internal Revenue Service, the SEC, and two divorce cases."

"What is the SEC?"

"Sorry. The SEC refers to the Securities and Exchange Commission. The SEC was created by the Securities Exchange Act of 1934. It has the legal authority to prescribe accounting methods for firms whose shares of stock and bonds are sold to the investing public on the stock exchanges. For the most part, the SEC has followed the standards established by the FASB concerning the methods used to develop the required information. However, after Sarbanes-Oxley a five-person Public Company Accounting Oversight Board (PCAOB) sets the standards for auditing of public companies."

"What is the FASB?" the young-looking lawyer asked.

"FASB stands for the Financial Accounting Standards Board that began to issue standards in 1973. The SEC has charged this seven-member independent, nongovernmental body with the responsibility of developing and issuing standards of financial accounting affecting the private sector of the United States. The FASB is our current source of Generally Accepted Accounting Principles for which accountants use the acronym GAAP."

Dr. Cramer continued. "In 2007, the SEC decided to allow non-U.S. firms listed on the U.S. stock markets to use International Financial Reporting Standards, acronym IFRS, instead of using U.S. GAAP. The IFRSs are issued by the International Accounting Standards Board. Its acronym is IASB."

The well-dressed attorney turned to the judge and said, "Your honor, we present to this court Dr. Cramer, as an expert witness in the area of forensic accounting and auditing."

The robed judge turned to the opposing attorney and said, "Counselor, do you have any objections to this request?"

The opposing attorney stood up and spoke loudly, "No, your honor."

"So moved. You may proceed, counselor."

Lenny answered a number of technical questions asked by his friendly attorney that he had previously rehearsed. Much of the material was in his written report prepared for the trial. Then the opposing attorney began his cross-examination. His questions focused on audit samplings for tests of transactions. The class-action negligence battle was brought by shareholders of QQQQ, Inc., an electronics-store chain, against their accounting firm, Peat, Andersen & Whinney. The chain's former management was accused of creating "phantom" inventory and profits.

"Now, Dr. Cramer, would you tell the court how an auditor statistically determines if the accounting records of a firm like QQQQ, Inc., are correct?"

"Most audit evidence is gathered during the two fieldwork stages: one, the internal control testing phase and two, the account balance-testing phase. During the internal control testing phase, the auditor gathers evidence while testing the internal controls to determine if reliance can be placed upon the controls. Auditors apply auditing procedures to obtain reasonable assurance that the financial statements are free of material misstatement. Auditing procedures also must include procedures to detect fraud."

Cramer continued. "Compliance tests are used to verify that a particular control procedure is working properly. For example, many business firms have procedures to ensure that they don't pay twice for the same order of goods from a vendor. On the average, companies double-pay their account payables by as much as 2 percent." Looking at the jurors, Cramer said, "I'm sure none of us wish to pay our bills twice." He turned and looked at the judge.

Generally, this protective procedure would involve accumulating documents like the purchase requisition, purchase order, receiving report, and the bill or invoice from the vendor. An example would be the utility bill that we receive each month. After comparing the data on all these documents to verify agreement, then a payment voucher would be prepared. All these documents would be forwarded to the firm's treasurer for check preparation. When the check is prepared, all these documents would be stamped 'paid.'"

Cramer paused to take a sip of water from the glass he had poured earlier. "The procedure I just described would ensure that if a business receives two bills for the same order, that the firm does not pay both times. The process also ensures that only goods actually ordered and received are paid for. The process of accumulating the documents into a voucher package and stamping them 'paid' when the check is written is a control procedure which an auditor may choose to test."

The attorney looked puzzled. "Are you saying, Professor Cramer, that the auditor may not test this procedure?"

Cramer was not surprised by this question. He thought to himself, "The general public knows so little about the true purpose of an audit. Perhaps worse than the public's mere ignorance was the public's misperception of what an audit is supposed to do. That misperception is usually referred to as the 'expectations gap.'"

"Professor Cramer, please answer the question." The attorney broke Cramer's train of thought.

"No, the auditor does not have to test any particular internal control procedure, only those upon which the auditor chooses to rely. Depending on the firm's unique situation, the auditor may rely upon many or no controls. After the auditor reviews the internal control system, a requirement of any audit, then the auditor selects those controls upon which he or she plans to rely. These controls will then be tested to see if they are functioning properly. The extent to which the auditor can rely upon these controls will determine the extent of the auditor's substantive tests."

"Professor Cramer, could you explain substantive tests?"

"Substantive tests also are referred to as tests of detail. A former Chief Auditor for the PCAOB, Doug Carmichael, called it 'shoe leather work.' You test all of the invoices or checks in a small area. The purpose is to detect material misstatements in the client's financial statements. The auditor must design substantive tests to determine if recorded book values are reasonably stated or if they are materially misstated. For example, a substantive test may estimate the dollar error in an account balance or class of related transactions, such as the dollar error in the accounts receivable balance or in the recorded total for sales. They also may be used to estimate an unknown account balance."

Lenny paused for a moment to catch his breath and then continued. "The quantity and quality of substantive tests are related to the field work standards. The first standard of field work mandates that substantive tests be adequately planned and properly supervised. The second standard requires that the nature, extent, and timing of substantive testing be based on the assessed level of control risk. The third standard requires that substantive tests contribute to the necessary sufficient competent evidence upon which to base an opinion regarding the financial statements under investigation."

"Now the risk that the auditor will reach the wrong conclusion is comprised of three separate risks: environmental risk, control risk, and detection risk. Perhaps I can discuss these risks later." Lenny looked directly at the attorney.

"As I was saying, however, before performing substantive tests, the auditor reviews the internal control structure, selects controls on which he or she plans to rely, and then tests those controls. The tests of controls are called compliance tests because these tests determine if the client firm's personnel are following, that is, complying with, the firm's stated control procedures. Keep in mind that management is responsible for establishing internal controls and attempting to stop fraud."

"Before we go any further, may I review the basic steps in the audit process?"

The attorney seemed to frowned, but said, "Go ahead."

"First, the auditor plans the audit. This step includes gathering information about the client's firm and industry conditions. Second, the auditor studies, tests, and evaluates the client firm's control structure. Third, the auditor performs and evaluates substantive tests. The second and third steps are the evidence-gathering steps of the audit. Audit working papers are used to document the auditor's techniques. Based upon this evidence, the auditor completes the fourth and final essential step, which is issuing the audit report."

Cramer continued. "This standard report includes what is referred to as an 'unqualified opinion,' which basically means that the financial statements are fairly presented. This standard report would be issued at the conclusion of any financial statement audit, unless there was a situation requiring a modification."

"Such as?" the attorney interrupted.

"There are basically two major situations requiring an opinion other than an unqualified opinion. One, if there is a limitation on the scope of the auditor's work. Two, if the financial statements are not prepared in accordance with accounting principles applied on a consistent basis. In performing the audit, the auditors must follow the auditing standard of PCAOB … Public Company Accounting Oversight Board."

"Please explain this scope limitation."

"As shown in their report, the auditor states that the audit was made in accordance with standards of PCAOB. The auditor must obtain reasonable assurance about whether the financial statements are free of material misstatements. In situations where the auditor does not follow PCAOB standards or is unable to perform auditing procedures which he or she considers necessary, the standard report must be modified to reflect this limitation in the scope of the auditor's work. The auditor can issue either a disclaimer or a qualified opinion. If the auditor disclaims an opinion because of a scope limitation, the audit report will contain only three paragraphs. The first paragraph would state that the auditor was engaged to audit the financial statements, which are the responsibility of management. A second paragraph would discuss the nature of the scope limitation. The third paragraph would disclaim an opinion. If the auditor disclaims an opinion, the auditor does not discuss what an audit is since this explanation may overshadow the disclaimer."

"The nature and potential effect of the scope limitation determine whether the auditor should issue a disclaimer or a qualified opinion. For an example of a disclaimer opinion due to a scope limitation assume that the client did not take a physical inventory of merchandise at year-end for 2008 and 2009 and that no evidence is available to support the cost of property and equipment acquired prior to December 31, 2008. Based on this information, the auditor's disclaimer of opinion might read as follows:"

> The company did not make a count of its physical inventory in 2009 and 2008, stated in the accompanying financial statements at $_____ as of December 31, 2009, and at $_____ as of December 31, 2008. Further, evidence supporting the cost of property and equipment acquired prior to December 31, 2008, is no longer available. The company's records do not permit the application of other auditing procedures to inventories or property and equipment.
>
> Since the company did not take physical inventories and we were not able to apply other auditing procedures to satisfy ourselves as to inventory quantities and the cost of property and equipment, the scope of our work was not sufficient to enable us to express, and we do not express, an opinion on the financial statements.

"If the auditor's scope is limited and the auditor decides not to disclaim an opinion, the auditor should issue a report which is qualified because of a scope limitation. A separate paragraph of the auditor's report would express an opinion that the financial statements are fairly presented in accordance with GAAP, except for any adjustments which may have been required had the auditor been able to complete the audit without any scope limitations."

Cramer paused to take two sips of water from his glass. "Departures from accounting principles can result in a qualified or an adverse opinion. Would you like further explanation?"

The attorney stared at Cramer for a couple of moments. "Not at this time. Let's go back to the issue of compliance tests and substantive tests. In particular, I would like for you to explain the statistical approaches that auditors use."

"Sure. But that's extremely complicated. Let's go back to my previous example of stamping the documents in the voucher package 'paid' when the check is prepared to pay the vendor's invoice. This procedure ensures that the firm only pays once for each vendor's invoice, and then only for goods which were actually ordered and received. The documents in the voucher package confirm goods were ordered, with the purchaser order, and confirm goods were received, with the receiving report. The person making out the payment voucher would examine these documents to be sure that they agreed with one another."

"If this procedure was not followed, the accuracy of the financial statements could be impaired. For example, the cost of goods sold amount on the income statement is often calculated by adding net purchases to beginning inventory and subtracting ending inventory. The amount of purchases is based on the payments to vendors for goods ordered. If those payments, that is, the checks, are not properly prepared, then cost of goods sold could be overstated or understated. Most likely overstated, since the vendors would probably complain if they did not receive payment for the goods shipped, but may not complain if they received over-payment."

Cramer paused and looked around the courtroom. He possessed a professor's habit of periodically making eye contact with his audience. Throughout his discussion he had been careful to look at the jurors, and not the lawyers. He wanted the jurors to think of him as a friend. He noticed that the judge seemed to be half-asleep. He sighed and started to continue his testifying. Before he could begin, his friendly attorney interrupted.

"Excuse me, Dr. Cramer. Your Honor, I would like to request a short recess."

The judge seemed to perk up a little bit. "A good suggestion. The court will recess for 15 minutes." He slammed the gavel. Everyone filed out of the courtroom. Most headed for bathrooms or concessions. Cramer went out of ear range of everyone and called Slam on his cell phone. Cramer could not have imagined what was happening at the other end of the phone connection.

"What am I doing?" Slam thought. He was leaning far out the window of his office when the ringing phone startled him. "Man, oh, man, I must be working too hard," he thought as he walked to his desk and picked up the phone.

"Slam, what took you so long?" came the voice over the phone even before Slam could say hello.

"Lenny, it's weird. I was daydreaming and looking out my window."

"Right, Slam. So you were daydreaming while I'm downtown busting my buns in a witness box at the courthouse. All the while, I'm counting on my colleague, Slam Duncan — computer whiz — to make some serious headway on our operational audit. I called to check in, and he tells me he's having a weird daydream!" Cramer's voice rose a few decibels as he finished his rebuff to Slam.

"No, no, you got this all wrong, Len. I think I'm seriously freaking out," Slam pleaded, although he was a little offended at Lenny's lack of compassion. Slam continued. "Your phone call must have brought me back to reality. I was leaning out the window, but I can't remember how I got there. In fact I can't remember what I was thinking. No, wait a minute. I remember ... I was flying. I thought I was a bird!"

"Weird, very weird, partner. You're sure you're really on the level?" Lenny became concerned. He felt bad about his initial gruffness. "But," he thought, "who wouldn't be a little grumpy after testifying in a courthouse all morning?"

Cramer continued. "Look, Slam, go over to your computer. Check out the program you're running. I think someone may be sending you subliminal suggestions."

"Now who's weird? Are you serious?"

"Yeah. I'm really serious. I've done some reading on the subject. A subliminal suggestion is a message flashed on a screen too fast for conscious reading. The television industry outlawed subliminal suggestions years ago. You may recall a Mission Impossible episode many years ago dealing with subliminal suggestion."

"Just go check out your computer. I have to go. I must get back to the courtroom. I will be cross-examined shortly."

Cramer hung up the phone and joined the crowd milling around outside the courtroom door. He had an uneasy feeling about Slam.

Just as everyone found their seats, the bailiff had everyone stand for the judge to enter the room. Lenny mentally prepared himself for the attorney's questioning.

"Professor Cramer, could you continue with your explanation of how auditors test control procedures. You were discussing the process of stamping the voucher package as 'paid.'"

"To test the control that the voucher package is stamped 'paid' before a check is issued, the auditor could retrieve each check and associated voucher package. If the stamp was missing, then the auditor would know the control procedure failed. That is, the client personnel did not follow the firm's stated internal control procedures."

"Due to the large number of transactions, the auditor would be unable to examine every transaction in the population of all purchase transactions. The cost of examining every transaction would be too huge for the firm to pay. The process of reaching a conclusion about an entire population based upon a sample has the fancy word extrapolation to describe it. Thus, to test the control, the auditor would select a sample of purchase transactions. The auditor would then retrieve copies of the associated voucher packages to determine if the documents were stamped."

"This type of sampling is known as attribute sampling. Here, the attribute being tested is the stamp on the voucher package documents. The auditor can use either *statistical* sampling or *judgmental* sampling. If statistical sampling is used, the auditor can mathematically determine the sample size by using either a formula, a graph, or a table, and randomly select the sample items. The auditor next investigates each sample item and prepares a working paper showing the results of the investigation. The auditor can then make a statistical conclusion about the effectiveness of a control procedure. Mathematical methods are used to determine sample size and to objectively justify its adequacy. This process means that the sample findings are free of unintended bias and defensible. The statistical approach provides a basis for expanding subsequent audit procedures if the results of a statistical test indicate that such expansion is necessary in the circumstances. Statistical sampling allows the quantification and control of sampling risks.

The attorney shuffled his papers and asked, "What do you mean by sampling risks?"

"Whether you use statistical or judgmental, that is, nonstatistical sampling, there are two types of sampling risk associated with attribute sampling, to test whether an internal control procedure is working effectively or not. They are: one, the risk of underreliance and two, the risk of overreliance. Underreliance risk is associated with the risk that sample results will indicate control ineffectiveness when in fact the true rate of breakdown is acceptable for the auditor's assessment of control risk. Auditors refer to the risk of underreliance as alpha risk. Auditors say that a Type I error results when a sample evaluation indicates that an effective control is ineffective."

"The risk of overreliance is defined as the beta risk, and a Type II error occurs when the sample evaluation indicates that an ineffective control is effective. The auditor does not know when a Type II error occurs because the auditor has erroneously concluded that a control is functioning properly. The opposite is true for a Type I error. That is, the auditor does not know when a Type I error occurs because the auditor has incorrectly concluded that a control is not working properly."

"In addition to sampling risks, there are nonsampling risks. These risks can be controlled by auditor competence, proper planning and supervision, and the CPA's adherence to appropriate quality control standards, The greater the degree of auditor competency, proper planning and supervision, and adherence to high quality control standards, the less the nonsampling risk."

"Allow me to go over a brief example of a compliance test using attribute sampling by continuing with our earlier example. Assume there are 5,000 purchase transactions each year, and an auditor wishes to determine that there is a stamped voucher package associated with each check disbursed. The auditor wishes to select a sample from the population of 5,000 transactions. Assume that the auditor wishes to be 95 percent sure of the result. In other words, there is a one in twenty chance that the sample will misrepresent the population. The acceptable level of detection risk is inversely related to the amount of audit evidence that the auditor plans to review. As the acceptable level of detection risk increases, the amount of necessary evidence gathering goes down."

"In addition to the reliability level, in this case 95 percent, the auditor also must specify the tolerable rate of occurrence, or TRO. In other words, the auditor must use professional judgment and determine how many deviations or lapses from the control procedure could occur without materially affecting the financial statements. Let us assume the auditor sets the TRO at 10 percent."

"Lastly, the auditor must estimate the expected rate of occurrence, or ERO. What error rate does the auditor expect to find? Typically, the ERO is based on prior experience, such as from previous audits. For my example, the auditor sets ERO at five percent."

"Tables exist to aid the auditor in determining sample size for attributes. Table 1 is an example. I would like to show two tables on my PowerPoint slides. This material is extremely complex." Cramer clicked on his computer, and he asked the judge if he could give copies of his slides to the jurors.

The judge thought for a moment and said, "Yes."

"Table 1 shows sample sizes for various tolerable rates of occurrence and various expected percentage rates of occurrence when the reliability is 95 percent. By examining this table, the auditor will determine that the sample size should be 120." Cramer had colored the 120 red and the 10 TRO green and 5.0 ERO green.

"Assume the auditor randomly samples 120 payroll calculations and finds errors in six calculations—a 5 percent sample occur-

Table 1

Determination of Sample Size
When Reliability = 95 Percent

Expected
percent
rate of
occurrence

Tolerable rate of occurrence

	1	2	3	4	5	6	7	8	9	**10**	12
0.50	*	320	160	120	100	80	70	60	60	50	40
1.0		600	260	160	100	80	70	60	60	50	40
2.0			900	300	200	140	90	80	70	50	40
3.0				*	400	200	160	100	90	80	60
5.0						*	500	240	160	**120**	80
7.0								*	600	300	140
10.0											800
15.0											
20.0											

* = MORE THAN 1,000.

Note: This table is exact for sampling with replacement and is a conservative approximation for sampling without replacement. It is designed for large populations where sample size is less than 10 percent of the population.

rence rate. Once an auditor has found the rate of occurrence in the sample, other tables are consulted to determine the achieved upper precision limit given the specified reliability. Specifically, Table 2 can be used to evaluate the findings." Cramer showed the second slide.

"In my example, the sample size is 120, so find 120 in left-most column of Table 2; the number of occurrences is 6; find 6 in the same row that has sample size of 120. Thus, the upper precision is 10 percent, which is found at the top of the column containing occurrence rate of 6. Thus, the auditor can be 95 percent confident that the population error rate will not exceed 10 percent. This percentage is same as the 10 percent originally deemed to be tolerable." Cramer paused for a moment.

"The other type of audit tests, substantive tests, are associated with variables sampling. Auditors use attribute sampling for compliance testing of control procedures. Variables sampling is used for substantive testing to estimate the dollar reasonableness of a fi-

Table 2

Evaluation of Sample Results Where
Reliability is Present at 95 Percent

NUMBER OF OBSERVED OCCURRENCES (DEVIATIONS)

UPPER PRECISION LIMIT:
PERCENT RATE OF OCCURRENCE Sample

Size	1	2	3	4	5	6	7	8	9	10	12
30										0	
60					0			1			02
100			0		1		2	3	4		06
120			0	1		2	3	4	5	**6**	08
200		0	1	3	4	6	7	9	11	12	16
300	0	1	3	6	8	11	13	16	18	21	26
500	1	4	8	12	16	21	25	29	34	38	47

Note: This table is exact for sampling with replacement and is a conservative approximation for sampling without replacement. It is designed for large populations where sample size is less than 10 percent of the population.

nancial statement account balance or the amount of material misstatement if the account is not reasonably stated. Auditors may use several types of variables sampling plans in conducting an audit. No one type of sampling plan is appropriate in all circumstances."

"Auditing standards describe the risks associated with substantive testing. The audit risk, abbreviated 'AR,' that is related to an individual account or class or transactions on the financial statements is the product of three risks. One, the environmental factors, before evaluating the functioning of internal control, that will lead to a material error — 'inherent risk,' abbreviated IR. Two, that the system of internal control will not prevent material error or detect it on a timely basis — 'control risk,' abbreviated CR. Three, that the auditor's procedures will fail to identify a material error not identified by the internal control system — 'detection risk,' abbreviated DR." Cramer held up fingers as he stated the three risks. The audit risk formula is therefore: AR = IR x CR x DR." Cramer showed the formula on a slide.

Cramer paused to clear his throat. "If you will bear with me, I have two more PowerPoint slides. These slides show how the auditor selects a variable sample to estimate the difference between a firm's recorded book value for an asset, such as inventory, and its true value. Please look at my handouts if you wish."

"Suppose an auditor has been assigned a variable sampling job to determine the reasonableness of a client's inventory balance. The auditor has previously observed the year-end count and was satisfied as to the count and the summarization of the count on the inventory summary sheets. The auditor prepares an audit program in which she randomly selects a sample of inventory items listed on the inventory summary sheets and traces those items to appropriate vendor invoices, comparing the unit prices on the inventory summary sheets with the unit prices on the vendor invoices." Cramer paused and drank some water.

"The auditor, in the audit program, specified the risk levels for incorrect rejection (alpha) and incorrect acceptance (beta) at 20 and 20 percent, respectively, and decides that the tolerable amount of error in the account should be 5 percent of the inventory account balance. Based on the prior year's working paper, a $10 standard deviation of differences is to be used in calculating the sample size. The standard deviation simply refers to variability."

"The auditor uses the sample to estimate the difference between the client's recorded values and the audited values. This difference is then used to estimate the true value of the population. Here, that's inventory. The formula for calculating the sample size for the difference estimator is as shown on my next slide."

$$n = [s(Z_{alpha} + Z_{beta})/(Min/N)]^2$$

where:

n	=	sample size
s	=	estimated sample standard deviation
Z_{alpha}	=	factor from the normal table for a two-sided alpha risk (risk of incorrect rejection)
Z_{beta}	=	factor from the normal table for a one-sided beta risk (risk of incorrect acceptance)
Min	=	minimum amount considered material
N	=	population size

Cramer continued his testimony. "I understand that this is difficult stuff. The first item needed is the standard deviation, in this case, $10. Next, we need the Z-values for alpha and beta risk. Alpha risk is a two-sided test. Thus, we look up the Z-value in the table of Z-values associated with the area under the normal curve. To do this, we would take half the alpha risk, in this case, half of .20 or .10, and subtract that from half the area under the curve or .50. The result is .40. When we look up the Z-value associated with .40, the answer is 1.28."

The attorney looked puzzled. "Professor, I studied statistics many years ago. Tell us what is a Z-value."

"Good question. Remember, a standard deviation refers to variability. Technically, it is the square root of the arithmetic average of the squares of the deviations from the mean in a frequency distribution. The Z-value is the number of standard deviation units associated with a given area under the normal curve from the mean value. For example, plus or minus three standard deviations from the population mean of a normal distribution include 99.9 percent of the population values, plus or minus two standard deviations includes 95.4 percent, and plus or minus one standard deviation includes 68.3 percent."

The attorney still looked puzzled, but nodded his head. "Please continue."

"The Z-value for the beta risk is a one-sided test. Thus, you subtract the whole beta risk amount, 20 percent, from .50. The result is .30. Consequently the Z-value for the beta risk is 0.84. Depending on the level of alpha and beta risk the auditor wishes to use, these Z-values will vary."

Cramer paused. He noticed that the jurors had disinterested looks on their faces, but he continued with his testifying anyway. He had lost them. Not good. "The next item in the formula is the minimum amount the auditor considers material. Let us assume the inventory is listed at $100,000. Thus, five percent is $5,000. Also, let us assume the population size is 2,000 items. By inserting these amounts in the sample size formula, the sample size is determined to be 72 items. The auditor would then select 72 items from among the population of 2,000 items to estimate the difference between the true value and the client firm's recorded value. The auditor will not look at all 2,000 items."

Cramer stopped. He thought, "These people have no idea what I'm talking about. Oh well, I have to try. He knew that a good expert witness had to make confusing, complex, and boring stuff interesting and easy to understand." He had explained to his attorney that this material was too complex for the courtroom, and his client-attorney had listened. He smiled. "Good thing I prepared these slides for the attorney."

His lawyer had said, "We will build you up as an expert. If the jurors believe you are an honest expert, we'll win."

The attorney asked, "Could you continue this example all the way to the auditor's conclusion?"

"Gladly. Assume the auditor takes this sample of 72 items and compares his audited value to the client's recorded book value for each item. The auditor determines that the book value of all 72 items is $720 more than the total audited value. Thus, the estimated population difference is calculated by multiplying the average difference of $10 by all 2,000 items in the population. The auditor's point estimate value for the population would be the book value of $100,000 plus the difference of minus $20,000. In this case the auditor's point estimate value is $80,000. However, to quantify the probability of this being the true value of the inventory, the auditor must establish a precision interval around this point estimate. If any of you have a question, please ask." He slowly looked at each juror and the judge. No one said anything.

"Now to calculate the precision interval, we must know the standard deviation of the sample. Assume this standard deviation is determined to be $9. This amount is used to calculate the standard error. You divide the standard deviation by the square root of the sample size—in this case, the square root of 72. The standard error is, therefore, $1.06. The formula for the precision interval is N, meaning population size, times the Z-value for alpha risk times the standard error. Here, the precision interval is 2,000 times 1.28 times $1.06, which equals $2,715. Thus, the auditor concludes with 80 percent confidence, that the true inventory value is $80,000 plus or minus $2,715."

Cramer looked at the jurors. "Since the client's recorded book value of $100,000 is not within the decision interval, $82,715 to $77,285;

the auditor must statistically conclude with 80 percent reliability that the inventory account is not reasonably stated." Cramer emphasized not.

"Thank you for that complicated lecture on statistics, Professor Cramer. I feel confident that all of us have benefited." "But I have three more questions. First, did these auditors plan and perform an appropriate audit to obtain reasonable assurance that the financial statements were free of material misstatements."

"Absolutely," Cramer responded. "I found that the auditors fully documented their tests, especially their test objectives, population attributes, calculation of sample size, evaluation of sample items, and disposition of discrepancies."

"Who is responsible for stopping and finding fraud in a business?"

"Management, of course," Cramer spoke loudly.

"So the external auditor is not required to find all fraud, such as stealing and cooking the books?"

"No. They are not required to find fraud. That's, of course, a major misconception of the public. This misconception is called the expectation gap. The internal auditors should have a better chance to find fraud."

"The internal auditors are different than the external auditors? Right?"

"You are absolutely correct. Internal auditors work for the business."

The attorney then turned to face the judge. "Sir, I am finished with this witness."

The judge looked at his watch. "The court will recess for an hour for lunch." The judge's gavel slammed, and the judge abruptly left the courtroom. He appeared to have heard enough about audit sampling.

As Cramer was leaving the courtroom, he knew that the jurors and judge did not understand his statistics. Too much technical jargon is deadly on the witness stand. Maybe they would remember the last four questions. Maybe they would believe that he was truly an expert. Outside he called Slam on his cell phone. After one ring, Slam picked up the phone.

"Yes." Slam's voice came over the phone line. Cramer breathed a sigh of relief.

"That you, Len?"

"You got him. So you didn't fly out the window. Was the computer involved in your odd behavior?"

"You were right, Sherlock. I used a memory-resident program. That's a program that runs concurrently with another program. I used the memory-resident program to slow down processing of the program I was running before my daydream. That's when I saw it. Parts of the subliminal message would appear on the screen for a split second. When the program ran at normal speed I couldn't see it. But when I slowed down the processing speed, there it was."

"Was what? What was the message?"

"You can fly. Soar like an eagle."

"And you believed that!" Cramer laughed now that he was no longer worried.

"The amazing part is how the hacker managed to get this message to appear mixed in with the program I was running. This message would appear only a word or two at a time along with pictures."

"Pictures?"

"Yeah. Pictures of birds in flight. I guess I thought I was ready to join them. You know, Lenny, this is one unusual audit. I'm not sure you're paying me enough. We accountants should get combat pay. By the way, the same subliminal message was on your computer."

Cramer chuckled. "I don't believe subliminal messages work. We'll talk about your pay later. Besides, maybe we'll write a good novel when we catch the bad guy. I have to get back to the trial." He paused. "Slam, I'm glad you're all right. See you later."

"Okay."

They closed the phones connections simultaneously.

Cramer didn't feel much like eating, but needed to kill some time before returning to the courtroom. He walked outside the building and found a little bookstore. He browsed there for a while. He purchased a copy of Leonard J. Brooks' *Business & Professional Ethics for Directors, Executives, & Accountants.* Afterwards he bought a sandwich at a delicatessen. As he ate, he wondered who had sent the subliminal messages to Slam.

Following his light lunch, he returned to the courthouse. Shortly, everyone involved had resumed their former positions in the courtroom, and he started the cross-examination.

The opposing attorney asked, "How much is your attorney paying you for your opinion in this dispute?" He turned to the jurors. "You're into this for the money. Right?"

Cramer knew that this question was frequently asked by an opposing attorney on cross-examination. He said, "I am not being paid for my opinion. I am being paid for my time, my expertise, and my experience. As you recall, for my disposition time, you paid for that seven hours."

"Okay, how much per hour are you being paid?"

"$350 per hour. However, that is less than what I am paid for my other consulting practice. Also, as a professor, I like to keep up with the practical side of the accounting profession. As a forensic accountant, I like to testify in the courtroom and try to get at the truth. I try to be an advocate for the truth."

The opposing attorney whispered to the assisting attorney on her left and then turned back to Cramer, and began her cross-examination. "Professor Cramer, help me out with a calculation. Assume the client firm has inventory stated at $4,039,000. The auditor wishes to estimate the inventory value based on the following sample data. One, the sample size is 100; two, the standard deviation of the sample is $200; three, the mean of the sample is $4,000; and four, there are 1,000 items in the population. Shouldn't the auditor reject the recorded book value if it's not between $4,000,000 plus or minus $25,600?"

Cramer pulled out a pencil, a piece of paper, and his calculator. "I'll need to use my calculator." He put in the formula: 1,000 times 1.28 times $200 divided by the square root of 100. The result was $25,600. He said, "Yes, the precision interval is plus or minus $25,600."

The plaintiff's attorney smiled. So did the assistant attorney. Cramer was puzzled by their expressions of apparent satisfaction.

"So, Professor, the auditors are wrong if they accept a recorded book value of $4,039,000?" The attorney's face had a look of pleasant anticipation, but she quickly replaced the smile with a frown when Cramer answered.

"No, no. I see what you're driving at. But the auditor may not have made a mistake accepting a value of $4,039,000. He may have used a different confidence level than 80 percent, such as 90 or 95 percent. The Z-value, also called reliability coefficient, is 1.28 for 80 percent confidence, 1.65 for 90 percent, and 1.96 for 95 percent. If you use the 95 percent confidence level, then the auditor would derive a wider precision interval than 80 percent. Let's see … It would be 1,000 times 1.96 times $200 divided by the square root of 100." Cramer turned and politely smiled at the jurors.

Cramer entered the amounts into his calculator. "Finally he said slowly, "The answer is $39,200. Thus, $4,039,000 would be between auditor's upper precision limit of $4,039,200 and lower precision limit of $3,960,800."

The plaintiff's attorney shook her head. "This math is really confusing me. How could an auditor reach different conclusions using the same data?"

"Let me please explain. By widening the decision interval from plus or minus $25,600 to plus or minus $39,200, the auditor increases the confidence level from 80 to 95 percent. The real question the auditor must ask is whether plus or minus $39,200 is sufficiently accurate. But being 80 percent confident that the true value is between $4,000,000 plus or minus $25,600 is equivalent to being 95 percent sure that the true value is between $4,000,000 plus or minus $39,200."

A light seemed to go on inside the attorney's head. She looked disappointed. "Okay, I see your point. The auditor could accept the $4,039,000 value depending on how precise he needed to be."

"Correct."

The attorney continued, "Well, how does the auditor determine the level of precision required?"

"In auditing we use a term called materiality. Materiality relates to the maximum amount a financial statement item could be misstated without affecting a financial statement user's decision process. Precision in statistical sampling corresponds to materiality. For example, consider a scenario in which an investor is considering purchasing stock in a firm with the inventory amount we just discussed — that is, $4,000,000. The question that the auditor must ask is what is the minimum amount of change that would affect the investor's decision. Would a change of $25,000 affect the investor's decision? $30,000? $40,000? $400,000? The answer is the level of materiality."

Cramer took a sip of water. "If the level of materiality is determined to be $40,000, then the auditor must conduct the audit to ensure at least that degree of accuracy."

"Wait a minute, Professor Cramer, how does the auditor determine this level of materiality? It seems very important as it corresponds to precision in statistical sampling?"

"An excellent question, and there is no easy answer. A CPA must exercise professional judgment in determining the level of materiality. Depending on each client's unique situation, the level of materiality may be different among audits by the same CPA firm."

"Nicely put, Professor. We're all interested in the truth here, but some things about auditing seem a bit subjective. They depend on judgment. How does the auditor gain this professional judgment? By passing the CPA exam?"

"Not exactly. Passing the CPA exam is the first step. However, to become a licensed CPA, one also must attain a certain level of experience. One or more years of work under the supervision of a CPA are required. The experience requirement varies from state to state. We have continuing education requirements just like lawyers."

"How can you be sure that a CPA firm is exercising good professional judgment in statistical sampling, and in conducting the audit, in general?"

Cramer shrugged off a feeling of defensiveness. He knew it was the attorney's job to question the work of CPAs who conducted the audit. If the CPAs were found negligent in conducting the audit, then the attorney and his clients — the ex-stockholders — would win the lawsuit.

"A quality review program is required for auditors of publicly traded companies."

"Who performs this review?"

"The Public Company Accounting Oversight Board handles these review programs. PCAOB was created by the Sarbanes-Oxley Act. Do you wish me to talk about PCAOB?"

"No thanks, professor. You've made your point."

"You always testify for defendants. Is that a fair statement?"

"No. I testify for plaintiffs as well. If you'll allow me to consult my resume I will point out the plaintiffs. I always try to be objective and impartial."

"That will not be necessary," the attorney quickly answered.

"Dr. Frank Sampton has a Ph.D. from Harvard University, and he testified that this CPA firm did commit accounting malpractice. He has quite an impressive resume with more than eighty-four publications, including two books. Would you agree that he is more qualified in this dispute than you are, and will you defer to his extensive background?"

"You have asked a compound question. Which should I answer first?" Cramer politely asked.

"Both." The attorney appeared shocked.

"While Dr. Sampton has an impressive resume, I have a great deal more practical experience. I have spent eight months studying the facts and evidence, and I believe the CPA firm did not commit malpractice. They handled the engagement in a professional and competent manner. I believe the jurors will determine that I am the most qualified expert in this dispute. He should defer to me, since he has so little practical, auditing experience."

Cramer paused. "I reviewed the CPA firm's working papers, which is the evidence compiled by an auditor during the audit engagement. According to Dr. Sampton's expert report, he failed to review the working papers. As Professor Ricchiute states in his auditing textbook, 'the quality of working papers is consequential, because the papers provide the principal support for an auditor's opinion, demonstrate compliance with PCAOB, and aids an audit team in performing and reviewing work.'"

Cramer looked into the eyes of some of the jurors. "In the liability literature, experts understand that working papers are the principal evidence for an auditor's due diligence defense under the Securities Acts. Along with studying the audit working papers, I reviewed the correspondence file, the permanent file, and the tax file in fulfilling my duties as an expert witness. As I tell my students, defeating fraud is a marathon, not a sprint."

"This CPA firm's working papers included evidence that they—" Cramer counted on his fingers for emphasis.

"One. They adequately planned, supervised, and reviewed. The first standard of field work."

"Two. They considered internal controls as a basis for planning substantive tests. The second standard of field work."

"Three. They obtained sufficient competent evidential matter. The third standard of field work."

Cramer shifted in the chair. "Even your expert under disposition admitted that the CPA firm met the General Standards. One. The audit was performed by persons having adequate technical training and proficiency." Cramer put up one finger.

"Two. In all matters relating to the assignment, independence in mental attitude was maintained by the auditors." Cramer put up two fingers.

"Three. Due professional care was exercised in the performance of the examination and the preparation of the report." Cramer put up three fingers.

The opposing attorney did not seem happy with Cramer's dissertation on working papers. However, Cramer felt that he had scored some valuable points with the jurors and judge, especially after his boring and complex sampling testimony.

A few more minor questions followed before Lenny's testimony was complete. From his previous experience as an expert witness, he had learned to restate the interrogator's question to suit his own purpose. He was pleased that things had gone so smoothly.

Cramer waited in the courtroom until the next break, and then he hailed a cab to go to his office at Georgia State University. On the way he read an article on expert systems for auditors in *Internal Auditing*. Expert systems were just one of the computer tools available to assist auditors. He was planning a class lecture on the topic. He recalled expert systems were the subject of Slam's dissertation. After his recent experience, however, Slam might wish to consider the topic of subliminal persuasion.

Chapter 10

When the [accounting] profession does things right, it's
not noticeable. When things go awry, that's news.

— Jack Ciesielski

Slam was in a terrible emotional state. He knew what the problem was. He had moved into the realm of love with Laura.

Yes, the state beyond liking. Sure he had liked several other
women. But not love. Not that totally vulnerable world of love.
Slam spoke out loud. "I'm not a teenager. Why can't I handle this?
Because love is a dangerous emotional feeling. Dangerous?"

He was now actually hearing the words in the songs on the radio.
That was a new experience for Slam. When he heard certain songs,
he would think of Laura and his chest would swell up. If he were
driving down Martin Luther King Freeway and heard love songs, he
would begin waving his hand and arm in rhythm with the music.
Yes, dangerous if someone thought he was motioning to them.

Slam was awaking earlier in the morning. He would wake up in
the middle of the night. He needed less sleep. Was this a common
reaction to love? Besides, what was love? Slam began composing
an e-mail letter to Laura on his computer.

"I am entering the world of love. It is a totally new experience
for me. I have no ground rules. I do not know how to behave." He
stopped for a moment.

"Please be understanding," he continued typing. "I may do something stupid or silly in my efforts to impress you. Please forgive me
if I do."

Slam stopped typing and read what he had written. He punched
the delete button. Why was he afraid to put his emotions into an

e-mail? Afraid of blackmail? Unmanly? Too frightening? Too exposed?" He knew that e-mails were the cockroaches of mass communication. They are there forever. Most white-collar criminals were sent to jail because of e-mail evidence.

Slain had tried before to express his emotions to Laura. He had cut out some pictures and cartoons from the newspaper. He had folded several pieces of white paper and made a booklet. On the front he wrote "Top Secret." Inside he drew a funny face with the statement "Slam likes Laura." Besides a clipping of two shoes, Slam wrote "I would walk 100 miles for Laura." He made little trails of red dots around the shoes. One of the trails of dots ended with the statement "I got lost here."

* * *

Cramer had precious little break time between the Coke audit and his auditing class at Georgia State, not to mention his serving as an expert witness. When he did have a spare minute he tried to catch up on the local news by reading the paper. The feature story in the Atlanta Constitution was a perennial one — abortion. Atlanta had received quite a bit of notoriety on the issue.

Thinking about the peaceful protesters brought back memories of Cramer's early days. His old friend, Will Posey, had been involved in the Civil Rights movement. Many years had elapsed since those carefree college days. It was interesting how Will had brought them back together by hiring him to do the operational audit for Coke.

He had first met Will at a conference for collegiate accounting societies at the University of Illinois. By chance, he and Cramer were involved together in several workshops and immediately became friends. Cramer was an undergraduate accounting major at the University of Massachusetts in Amherst at the time. Will was attending Grambling State University, a predominantly black school in Grambling, Louisiana. Both Cramer and Will were highly enthusiastic about the field of accounting. Both had grand dreams about the future of the profession and the impact they personally would make. Later, they both were accepted to the M.B.A. program at Harvard. There they became truly close friends while learning to properly pronounce "hah-vuhd" and having numerous Boston adventures together.

Cramer went on to pursue a doctorate at the University of Illinois. After earning his Harvard M.B.A., Will accepted a job with the Internal Revenue Service. Later he switched to his present job with Coke. They stayed in touch through the years, mostly through Christmas cards. Cramer was suddenly jolted from his reverie when he realized it was time to leave for class.

* * *

Lenny Cramer hurried into the old, white block general classroom building. He was already late, so he did not have time to go to his office. Instead he headed toward the waiting auditing students. He wanted to talk about the seven types of audit evidence today: physical examination, confirmation, documentation, observation, inquiries from clients, mechanical accuracy, and analytical tests. As Cramer walked into his classroom he noticed that the Elmo projector was already on, and he chuckled when he saw a fallen down stick figure on the screen. It was labeled Lenny Cramer. Scrawled across the top of the screen was:

AUDITORS NEVER DIE
THEY JUST LOSE THEIR BALANCE!

Cramer then noticed a group of students at the front of the classroom. As he walked toward the front he asked loudly, "What's up, gang?"

Mary Ann, an older student, excitedly explained. "Professor Cramer, Jimmy just fainted." She pointed to a student lying in a heap on the floor.

Cramer rushed over, and felt for the pulse on the student's neck. There was no discernible pulse. Cramer next put his right hand on Jimmy's forehead. His head was cold. His skin had a bluish-gray cast—probably due to lack of oxygen.

"Has anyone called for an ambulance?" Cramer asked sharply. No one spoke. They seemed to be frozen in place.

Cramer turned to the nearest student and commanded, "Use a cell phone and call 911!"

As the student pulled out his cell phone, Mary Ann pointed to another student, and said, "When Dewayne and Jimmy went to the front to put on a sheet of paper to show a riddle, there was some white powder on the glass. Dewayne blew the powder off, and it got on Jimmy. Then Jimmy fell down."

Cramer had a habit of telling riddles to his classes. At those words, Cramer remembered the computer warning—Lenny Cramer, quit the audit or your next lecture will be your last. Someone had tried to kill him! One of his students may be dead instead.

Slam had received a warning also. What was it? Something about his turning on his computer. Would the culprit put the powder on Slam's computer? I've got to call him!

Cramer turned to Mary Ann. "I have to call someone immediately. Get everyone outside now." And Cramer emphasized the word "now." "Mary Ann, you wait outside the front door to the building for the paramedics and direct them here." The students began leaving the room. They were visibly shaken. What a way for his students to get a walk.

"Do you think it's cocaine?" Mary Ann asked.

"I doubt it." As Cramer waited beside Jimmy, he used his own cell phone to call Slam. Slam's cell phone immediately went to voice mail. Cramer tried Slam's office telephone at Coke. After fifteen rings, there was still no answer. He called Slam's apartment. No answer. Where was Slam? He futilely tried Slam's office again. He was at a loss of what to do next.

It's strange how one's mind will wander in stressful situations. Cramer noticed the poster on the wall of the classroom:

ONLY AN ACCOUNTANT COULD CATCH AL CAPONE

Infamous mobster Al Capone wasn't easy to catch. But when Special Agents of the IRS stepped in and charged him with tax evasion, this crime czar's career came to an end. Prison time. Proof that sometimes only the accountant can apprehend the criminal.

BE AN ACCOUNTANT WITH CONVICTION

It was an advertisement for an IRS Special Agent. Employees in the IRS were some of the first forensic accountants in the U.S. Cramer felt compelled to catch this madman who was now jeopardizing peoples' lives.

To Cramer's great relief, two medics rushed into the classroom. His relief was short lived. After determining that Jimmy wasn't breathing, the medics performed CPR, but it was to no avail. Jimmy was dead. The medics informed Cramer that they would call the police and the coroner. An autopsy would be performed. Cramer shuddered as he considered the full impact of this needless tragedy. He felt nauseated.

After Cramer told the paramedics about the white powder, he hurried to his car to drive to One Coke Plaza. He had to find Slam. He might be working late tonight.

* * *

Slam had heard the ringing of his cell phone and the office phone. They were loud. He was staring at the ceiling, while lying on the floor in his office. He could not move his arms and legs. He could not sit up. He could not speak or breathe. But he could hear and think.

When he came into his office ten minutes ago, he immediately saw something that looked like baby powder on his computer. He had first thought that the building custodians had tried cleaning his equipment. But then he recalled the warnings he and Lenny had received. Perhaps someone was trying to sabotage his computer.

He remembered taking a Kleenex and carefully wiping off the computer. After dusting most of the white powder from the keyboard, he flipped on his computer. When he made his first entry, a message flashed on the screen:

SLAM, YOU ARE NOW DEAD!

"Sure I am," Slam said. He felt faint, however. He moved his chair back from the computer, tried to stand, but fell backwards. His arms and legs were numb. That was about five minutes ago. The phone was ringing again. "Someone turn it off, please."

A person rushed into his office to pick up the phone. "Why don't you wake up and answer the phone, Slam?"

Alarmed, Laura spoke, "Wake up, Slam! Wake up!" Slam could see Laura, but he could not speak or move. He could not feel Laura's hands shaking him.

Laura walked back to his phone, dialed, and then said, "There has been an accident. Please call an ambulance and have the medics come to Room 423 in the Coke building. Slam Duncan is sick."

Slam heard Laura leave the room, but she returned shortly with a co-worker. He could hear them whispering—as if he was dead. "I'm not dead. I just can't *move*. Help me, please."

Soon two medics rushed into the room with a stretcher. The larger medic said, "What happened?"

"I came into Slam's office to answer his phone and found him on the floor. I don't know what happened."

The second medic bent over Slam and felt his throat.

"There's no pulse." Then the medic tore open Slam's shirt and listened for Slam's heartbeat. "Did anyone here try CPR?" When no one answered, the medic frowned. "Well, it's too late now. He's dead. He may have had a heart attack. You'll need to call the coroner."

"He's too young to die. Can't you take the body?" Laura pleaded.

"Nope. The coroner will have to declare him dead. You'll need an autopsy."

Everyone left. Slam tried to scream. He could not move. Soon he heard someone running down the hall into his office. "Slam. Oh, no. They've killed you too."

Cramer put his hand on Slam's forehead. "It's cold like the student. Where is the powder?" Cramer walked slowly around the office, stopping at the computer. He carefully looked at the system. He noticed that the screen was blank, although the computer was on. There was some white powder on the floor. Someone must have put powder on the keyboard. He was careful not to touch the white powder. Cramer sat down in a chair and waited. "I should have reported the threat." He dropped his head, feeling much remorse.

Cramer called the police. "Hello. This is Lenny Cramer. I wish to report two murders."

"Yes. Lenny Cramer. I'm calling from Room 423 in the Coke Building. I'll wait for you."

When the police officers arrived, Cramer told them about the white powder on the floor. He explained the related incident with his student. He also told them about the previous threats that he and Slam had received.

The police carefully gathered a sample of white powder and blocked off the area for the crime investigation team.

"Could you let me know what is this white powder?" Cramer asked.

"Sure. You'll remain in town, Dr. Cramer? Right?"

As they finished speaking, Laura walked into the room, followed by a man from the coroner's office. "Hello," she croaked to Cramer. She looked pale.

* * *

Slam was finally able to move in the morgue *before* the autopsy. But he had to remain in the hospital for two days.

The poison was tetrodotoxin, one thousand times more toxic than cyanide. This highly toxic poison is found in the reproductive organs and liver of the puffer fish found off the coasts of Japan.

The powder also contained bufotenine and bufotoxin, two ingredients from dried toad skins from Haiti. The frog skin ingredients enhanced the effect of the basic poison. Voodoo powder killed one student and almost killed Slam. He was lucky. He had been a zombie for *only* four hours.

Laura and Cramer visited Slam both evenings in the hospital. Cramer explained in detail the incident in his classroom. "My student died from the zombie poison. Do you think Don Ball is involved. Dan Mays?" Who else might be doing this madness? The trio had no firm answer, but they made a pact to find the killer quickly.

* * *

Soon after arriving at work in the Coke Building the next morning the phone rang on Cramer's desk. "Hello, this is Lenny Cramer."

"Lenny, would you like to meet for lunch today?"

Cramer immediately recognized the voice of Will Posey. Feeling worn-out from the two disasters, Cramer was tempted to decline the lunch get-together. However, he also felt a need to confide in someone. "Sounds good. What about Ling-Po's Chinese Restaurant?"

"Great. Can you meet me there a little before noon, say 11:30? That way we can beat the main lunch crowd."

Cramer glanced at his desk calendar to be sure he could. "Sure."

"See you then." There was a click as Will hung up.

Cramer decided to start a new direction in the forensic audit before leaving for lunch. He logged onto the mainframe from his personal computer. He pulled up the sales files. First, he looked at the monthly sales summary reports. These were broken down by domestic and foreign sales. He pulled up the foreign reports that were further categorized by individual countries. He briefly examined each country's sales summary.

The sales summary report contained the following information. First, the title of the report and time period covered appeared at the top. This information was followed by columnar headings: location, last month's sales, current month's sales, percent change, year-to-date sales, last year's year-to-date sales, and percent change. The location column listed various city locations throughout the given country. Significant percent changes, monthly or year-to-date, were marked by asterisks on the report. A separate attached report provided explanations or comments regarding these significant changes. For example, one comment was "increase in sales due to onset of tourist season."

After reviewing the most recent month's sales summaries for a number of foreign countries, Cramer noticed it was time to leave for lunch. He logged off, picked up his coat, and left his office. The restaurant was a reasonable walk from the Coke building, but he needed the exercise. He had just enough time to walk and make it to Ling-Po's by a quarter till noon. He set a fast pace weaving in and out of the lunch crowd.

As he entered the eating establishment he caught sight of Will sitting at a booth near the door. He glanced at his watch. The time was 11:40. Drat, he thought. He really hated being even a little late.

Will saw Cramer make his way to the booth. Both smiled wide. "Howdy, Len. You're looking sharp. Well, as sharp as a professor can look to someone who thought all professors were a bit crazy."

"Well, you look as good as a former IRS agent can to a disgruntled taxpayer."

"Touche! Don't tell me you're one of those nuts with a bumper sticker that says 'Stop Organized Crime, Abolish The IRS?'"

Cramer laughed. "Of course not, old friend. I'm well aware that it's the U. S. Congress that passes the tax laws. The IRS is just the collection agency. Why, I just didn't realize how sensitive you were after all those years of working for the IRS."

Will managed a weak grin. "Yeah. I reckon I've gotten more sensitive as the years have rolled by. Even though I work for Coke now and not the IRS, I'm sick and tired of people getting mad at the IRS and not their congressman. It's the people who keep electing tax-crazy politicians who make me the maddest. Well, you've gotten me off on a soapbox, and we haven't even ordered lunch yet!"

Cramer laughed again. "You always were one for soapboxes. You were out to change the world when we first met. I guess you still are."

"We've come a long way, Len. The world really has changed if you're referring to civil rights and Barack Obama. Unfortunately we still have a ways to go, if you're talking about accounting. Well, it's really incredible how much has changed—tax laws and the probable conversion to international standards. The country is lawsuit-crazy, and some accountants can't afford professional liability insurance. Of course, an ivory tower professor like yourself is probably unaware of these events." Will finished his comment with a chuckle. He always enjoyed kidding a friend, especially an old one like Cramer.

"Now, that's plain unfair. I'm not going to dignify that statement with a reply. Instead I'm changing the subject. How's the family? Everything seemed great the night we had dinner at your place."

"I'm happy to say that everything is going fine. Not much has changed since your visit. Emma is well. She really likes her job as a market researcher. The two girls are finding college especially challenging this semester. I think I told you that our oldest is an accounting major at the University of Georgia."

"Did her dear old dad influence her choice of major?"

"Not really. I suppose she was affected by my work. You know I really do like our field. There are a lot of options for an accounting graduate—public accounting, management accounting, taxation, and government jobs. I think she'll be happy in any one of those career paths."

They stopped talking to place their orders when the waiter came to their booth.

Will continued. "How do you like Atlanta? Has it been hard as a single parent?" Will paused. "That's a dumb question isn't it?"

"Well, we've managed fine. Sure, there have been some tough moments. Becc has adjusted well, though. I'm thankful for that. My consulting business is back in gear, thanks to your help at Coke. However, this operational audit at Coke is turning into my roughest job so far."

Will already knew about the murder of the student and near-murder of Slam. Cramer proceeded to tell him the details of the tragic murder of his student at Georgia State. During this dialogue, the waiter brought their food.

"We ran into some wackos occasionally during my IRS audit days, but not murderers," Will commented as he reached for the soy sauce. "Are you sure you want to continue this thing? There are other audits out there. Most of them are probably a lot less dangerous."

"No, I can't quit. This guy has got to pay. I intend to find out who he is. With Slam's help, plus your Coke colleague, Laura, I figure it's just a matter of time before we find him."

Will nodded his head. "Could be a woman. Equal opportunity, you know. You always were a determined fellow, Lenny." Will grinned.

The two men talked for another half an hour. When they finished, the waiter brought the check and two fortune cookies to the table.

"Well, look at this," Will stated as he read his fortune.

"It says 'Help, I'm being held prisoner in a Chinese fortune cookie factory.'" He laughed at his own joke.

"Funny," commented Cramer. "Mine says 'Beware of former IRS agents who eat at Chinese restaurants.'" Both men chuckled.

"Will, I have really enjoyed this lunch get-together. It really helps me to unload my recent disasters to a sympathetic ear. Becc and I would like to have you and your family over for dinner."

"Dinner sounds great. I'll check with Emma and get back to you, and you keep me posted on this murder investigation." The waiter walked over to pick up the check and payment. Both men reached for their wallets. "It's my treat," Cramer insisted. "I owe you a lot more than a lunch."

"Well, thanks old buddy. I guess you do." Will joked.

Cramer used his American Express card. "Don't leave home without it." He gave Will a comical look. "TV commercials are brain-washing us."

The two men walked back to the Coke complex and split up inside the building.

After returning to work, Cramer discovered an old newspaper clipping in one of his desk drawers. The former occupant had apparently clipped an article from a newspaper and left it in the desk. Out of curiosity, Cramer picked it up and began reading. The article described Coke's Super Bowl XXIII halftime show. Coca-Cola had arranged a 3-D commercial and halftime show.

The company had packaged the 3-D glasses with Coke products. A great deal of publicity had been given to Coke regarding the first live 3-D show and commercial in network history. Cramer recalled the January 1989 Super Bowl. It had been one of the best Super Bowls ever. San Francisco beat Cincinnati with a last minute touchdown pass by Joe Montana. Paul Harvey had even described the winning play in his daily radio show, "The Rest of the Story." It turned out that the players had gotten mixed up and run the winning play wrong. Cramer thought how funny that goof-ups can sometimes work out for the best. The last 3-D movie he had seen was the Journey to the Center of the Earth.

Cramer then returned to his examination of the Sales Summary Reports. He noticed that Coke had operations in a number of countries in Eastern Europe. He recalled that Slam and Laura were planning a trip to Poland together. Laura wanted to establish a Coke plant there, and Slam had arranged to accompany her on the trip to meet with some of the government officials. Since Slam's near-death incident, he had really hit it off with Laura. Cramer thought there was nothing wrong with that. He sometimes wished there was more romance in his own life. However, he felt he needed more time to adjust to his wife's death.

As he looked at the reports on his computer, he continued his earlier procedure to scan the "percent change" columns for the monthly sales changes and year-to-date sales changes. The significant percent changes were marked with asterisks. A separate attached report provided comments and explanations for these significant items. On one of these "comment" reports he saw a comment for the year-to-date change that he had not seen before — "same as last month." Since he had not read a "same as last month" explanation before, the oddity of it made him curious. Consequently, he pulled up the preceding month's report to see what had occurred at that time to cause a significant change in the year-to-date sales.

"Now this is getting interesting," said Cramer to himself as he looked at the prior month's sales report. On that report, as for the current month's report, there was no significant change from the prior month's sales, but the year-to-date sales were down by 70 percent from the prior year's year-to-date. And again, there was that explanation — "same as last month." Cramer pulled up the preceding month and again found the same explanation. He wondered, "How far back am I going to have to go to get an explanation other than 'same as last month?'" He pulled up the next prior month's report that was three months back from the current month's report, and found the same comment in both the monthly change and year-to-date change columns — "New machines. Not working properly."

Cramer realized his knowledge of Coca-Cola's dispensing machinery was rather limited, but that explanation just made him all the more curious. A red flag? He began wondering what else could explain the unusual change. "How could new machines cause a drop-off in the month's sales four months in a row? If there was a problem, it should have been fixed before now. However, it was in an Eastern European country. Perhaps, some local government official was actually causing the problem. Or perhaps, the local help was slow to fix an American firm's equipment." He made a note in his workpapers to investigate further, when his phone rang.

"I've got something," Slam Duncan said quietly into the receiver.

Cramer, on the other end responded. "I'll come down to your work center."

"No," Duncan retorted. "I'll come up to your office. It's in a quieter section of the building. More secure. This is big! I think I know whodunit."

"Well, don't delay! Get up here and tell me."

Chapter 11

The great composer does not set to work because he is inspired, but becomes inspired because he is working. Beethoven, Wagner, Bach, and Mozart settled down day after day to the job in hand with as much regularity as an accountant settles down each day to his figures. They didn't waste time for an inspiration.

—Ernest Newman

"Don't you get it, Lenny? This guy has to be our man. He's been retired for a few years, and he's beginning to feel pinched living on his fixed retirement income. Then, presto-whammo, he gets an idea—steal some valuable information from my old employer and sell it to a rival company."

"Whoa, buddy. I understand Doyle Loebbecke was in charge of programming when Coke installed their last system, but please explain again why you think he's the hacker."

"Ok. First of all, he's the only one with sufficient knowledge of the system to be able to do it. We know the hacker used a Trojan-Horse type of trap door to get into the system. Only a programmer with intimate knowledge of the system could do that. But to move around in the system would require more than just the getting-in kind of knowledge. It requires knowledge of additional passwords, and more importantly, how the system is configured. This guy would know that. But here's the clincher—he's using the same account number he had twenty years ago. I went back through the old master lists of valid user-IDs and related passwords since Coke got their first dial-in computer system. His old ID and password were there and match the ones the hacker used."

"Slam, gimme a break. He couldn't be that stupid. Why would he use a number that's bound to give him away?"

"I thought about that. Two reasons. One, it's twenty-years old. Who'd think to look through the old records except a genius like myself. Two, he's desperate and couldn't break into the system any other way. Also, we still can't prove he stole anything of value yet. All he has done is retrieve tons of inventory records data, primarily about shipments received. But here's where it gets interesting. I have a theory. Don't laugh."

Cramer smiled a crooked smile. "Laugh. I can't laugh. I can't wait for you to make sense of all of this for me."

"The Coke formula. He's after the Coke formula!"

The two men stared at each other for a few moments.

Cramer burst out laughing. "You're kidding me. Water, sugar, carbon dioxide, and the Seven X." He kept laughing.

"Don't laugh. In 2007, two Coke employees were sentenced to eight and five years in prison for conspiring to steal the Coke formula and trying to sell it to Pepsi. Pepsi told Coke, and Coca-Cola contacted the FBI, and a sting operation was initiated. Investigators found the bad guys through images from a security camera. Coca-Cola used this camera evidence to convict the people involved."

Cramer stopped laughing and said, "Okay. Tell me more." But he was still smiling.

Slam just stared at Cramer. "Don't you see. He's after the Seven X part of the formula. Listen to me. The inventory records are the key. Doyle Loebbecke worked for Coke for almost forty years. Don't you think he was aware of opportunities for industrial spying. This soft drink business is super-competitive. It's a war out there. Sure, Coke is number one, but they have some mean competitors, especially Pepsi. You've heard of the 'Pepsi Challenge' haven't you?"

Cramer was still skeptical. "You're serious, aren't you?"

"Dead serious. I think this is the guy who tried to kill me."

Cramer was taken aback by that statement. "All right. Let's assume you're right, just for the sake of discussion. How does he get the Coke formula from the inventory records? The formula is one of the most highly guarded corporate secrets in the world of corporate secrets. I reckon the Colonel's secret recipe of 11 herbs and spices is the only thing close in terms of major corporate secrets."

"Thanks for hearing me out," Slam responded with a bit of indignation. He was a bit miffed from Cramer's unnecessary laughter. "I didn't understand the significance of the inventory records at first myself, but as I pondered over it several nights, it finally occurred to me. Loebbecke is analyzing the records to derive the Coke formula."

"How?" Cramer asked.

"Elementary, Mr. Watson. Cost accounting. By accumulating years and years of records, and by being intimately aware of Coke's production cycles, Loebbecke can determine exactly what combination of ingredients is necessary to make the world's most popular soft drink. He can then sell the formula to the highest bidder in the industry."

"Pepsi?" Cramer responded.

"Perhaps. Or some newcomer to the soft drink field. Maybe to a foreign country. India. China. Remember India kicked Coke out a number of years ago. They have a similar cola, but it doesn't taste as good. Once in a while a new brand pops up. Most only last a few years. Rarely do any make a profit. People know Coke, and they just keep coming back to it after trying the no-names for a while."

"Well, you have me interested, Slam. India. It's quite a theory, but barely plausible. If all you say is true, why did Loebbecke unleash the virus into the system?"

"Elementary, my dear professor. Loebbecke found out about our audit, and he decided to cover his tracks. Did you know that the Coke system staff could not find back-ups to some of the destroyed files. Fortunately, yours truly had downloaded some of the crucial ones back at the beginning of our audit job, such as the old master lists of user-IDs and passwords I just mentioned."

"But what made him so desperate that he tried to kill us?" Cramer interrupted.

"I suppose he thought we were going to stop his money-making plans from coming to fruition. Maybe he thought our operational audit was aimed specifically at him. Maybe he just didn't like our looks. Maybe he doesn't like my mustache. But I have a plan to get some hard evidence to prove he's the hacker."

"Well, go on, don't leave me hanging."

Slam continued. "First, we arrange to have the phone lines monitored. Next time he logs on, we will have the call traced to his house. That's the main strategy. But being the resourceful guy that I am, I also have a back-up plan. I have the guy's address, and I'm gonna tap into his computer system."

"Tap in? You think he has a dial-in service on his PC?"

"I doubt it. But that's not how I'm getting into his castle." Slam lowered his voice to a whisper. "I purchased some electronic eavesdropping equipment, my friend. The stuff cost me $600. You'll see it on my next expense report. The equipment consists of a battery-powered '11' set, a TV antenna, and some basic electronic gear. Primarily a couple of oscillators."

"You're beginning to sound like James Bond. How does this spy stuff work?"

"Well, I plan to park in front of Loebbecke's house and tune into his PC's display screen. Most computer systems emanate electro-magnetic radiation from the circuitry and from their CRTs. The CRT — uh, that is, cathode-ray tube — is what shoots the beam of electrons that form the image on the monitor screen. My spy gear will allow me to pick up that signal. If all goes as planned, I'll be able to see exactly what Loebbecke sees on his screen. Also, I plan to record it on a portable VCR to further prove his guilt."

Slam paused in his monologue for Cramer's reaction. Cramer didn't say anything immediately, and Slam continued. "By the way, I'll need to rent a van to work from. My bike isn't big enough to hold all this gear, let alone to do my work secretly, if you know what I mean?"

Cramer began slowly smiling and shaking his head. "This audit is really getting crazy." He began humming the theme from the classic TV series, "The Twilight Zone." Slam joined in. They both laughed.

After discussing some practical details to the spy caper, Cramer and Slam said goodbye. Cramer meant to discuss the unusual sales summary report from the Polish location with Slam, but he forgot to bring it up during all of Slam's revelations regarding the former Coke executive. Well, he'd try to remember to tell Slam about it before he went overseas with Laura. "Was it legal to read Loebbecke's computer screen?"

Cramer looked at his watch. "Good grief," he thought, "I need to look over my notes about legal liability before driving over to the campus."

* * *

As Cramer entered the classroom, he knew it would be difficult to have a normal lecture so soon after Jimmy's tragic death. What really grieved Cramer was the fact that Jimmy had died as a result of the misfortune of being in Dr. Lenny Cramer's auditing class. None of the other accounting professors at Georgia State had provoked any homicidal maniacs.

Cramer could not bring back the dead student, but he would not rest until he found the student's killer. Cramer noticed on his class roster that Dewayne had dropped the class. Poor Dewayne would always feel guilty that he had been the one to blow the voodoo powder off the Elmo projector and onto Jimmy. Cramer decided that he would try to have a visit with Dewayne. After all, if anyone was to blame, Cramer thought, it wasn't Dewayne but Cramer himself.

He placed a sheet on the Elmo projector with some hesitancy, momentarily recalling it was one of the murderer's tools. He pointed to the screen behind him and said, "Today I will cover a number of miscellaneous topics. For example, an auditor must perform a walkthrough of a company's significant processes. In other words, an auditor must walkthrough each major class of transactions. This task can not be achieved secondhand."

Pointing to the PowerPoint slide on the screen, Cramer said, "According to PCAOB, in a walkthrough an auditor traces company transactions and events—both those that are routine and recurring and those that are unusual—from origination, through the company's accounting and information systems and financial report preparation processes, to their being reported in the company's financial statements."

"As an auditor, you should perform your own walkthrough, which will provide you as an auditor with appropriate evidence to make an intelligent assessment of internal controls. Asking intelligent questions is critical. Do not merely observe the employees but ask, 'what do you do when there is a problem?' Suppose the boss is not here to sign the check. What happens? You are searching for the situations where the internal controls are overridden."

"In past classes we have talked about the General Standards and the Field Work Standards of an auditor. Here are the Standards of Reporting." Cramer put up the four standards on the Elmo projector.

Standards of Reporting

1. The audit report shall state whether the financial statements are presented in accordance with generally accepted accounting principles (GAAP).
2. The report shall state whether such principles have been consistently observed in the current period in relation to the preceding period.
3. Informative disclosures in the financial statements are to be regarded as reasonably adequate unless otherwise stated in the report.
4. The report shall either contain an expression of opinion regarding the financial statements, taken as a whole, or an assertion to the effect that an opinion cannot be expressed. When an overall opinion cannot be expressed, the reasons therefore should be stated. In all cases where an auditor's name is associated with financial statements, the report should contain a clear-cut indication of the character of the auditor's examination, if any, and the degree of responsibility the auditor is taking.

"Keep in mind that a Certified Public Accountant should not escape liability if he or she fails to perform at or above reasonable standards," said Cramer.

A student raised her hand. "Yes," Cramer responded, nodding his head toward Sonya Thornhill.

"Professor, why do we read about so many accounting firms being sued? Are the employees incompetent?"

Cramer stopped for a moment. "Accountants are at risk. I believe auditors should get danger pay. According to Marc Epstein and

Albert Spalding, the U.S. legal system has turned its guns onto the accounting profession. As accountants are hammered with lawsuits, judgments, and settlements, the profession is itself at risk. I have placed on reserve in the library their excellent book, *The Accountant's Guide to Legal Liability and Ethics.* Essentially, CPA firms are 'deep pockets.' When a company goes bankrupt, the CPA firm may be the last one standing. Burnt investors and creditors often will look for the 'deep pocket.'"

"There was a four-year class-action lawsuit brought by shareholders after the Tyco International approximately $5.8 billion accounting fraud. Although the investors losses were between $1 to $2 billion, PricewaterhouseCoopers agreed to pay $225 million and Tyco agreed to pay $2.975 billion. This total settlement of $5.2 billion was reached after extensive litigation and mediation."

"Several types of lawsuits may be brought against accountants." Cramer wrote on the blackboard.

- Breach of Contract.
- Negligence (a tort).
- Fraud.
- Violation of securities laws.

"For a tort, a professional has a duty to exercise the level of care, skill, and diligence normally performed by other members of a profession under similar circumstances. For example, to prove negligence—a tort—a party must prove the following:

- There was a misrepresentation.
- Of a material fact.
- To a party whom an accountant owes a duty.
- And the plaintiff justifiably relied.
- Proximate cause of the damage."

"Proximate cause generally includes two elements.

- Cause in fact;
- Foreseeability.

"An accountant's third-party risk depends upon the states, since there are basically four approaches to third party liability:

- **Restrictive privity** (Pa. and Va.) requires direct connection between an accountant and another party. So you wish to get a job in these two states.
- **Near-privity approach** (about 17 states). Releases accountants from mere blunders.
- **Restatement Second approach** (about 21 states). Middle-of-the-road; intended beneficiaries.
- **Reasonable foreseeability** approach (Miss. and Wisconsin). Almost endless."

"In general, plaintiffs have three strategies as they go after auditors:

1. The financial statements are wrong. The auditors did not follow GAAP.
2. Accountants did not perform their duties. They did not follow GAAS or PCAOB.
3. The auditors should have found the problems. In other words, they ignored the red flags."

"Accountants generally have these defensive strategies.

1. But the statements were accurate.
2. There was no justifiable reliance.
3. SODDIT: Some Other Dude Did It. Others were at fault.
4. The audit report does not say the numbers are correct.
5. Statute of limitations have passed.
6. These were a mere error in judgment."

"O.K. You are on your first audit job. I want you to remember what the Panel of Audit Effectiveness suggested in 2000. They recommended that surprise or unpredictable elements should be incorporated into audit tests, including." Cramer put another sheet onto the Elmo.

- Recounts of inventory and unannounced visits to locations.
- Interview of financial and non-financial client personnel in different locations.
- Requests for written confirmations from client employees regarding matters about which they have made representations to the auditors.

- Tests of accounts not normally performed annually.
- Tests of accounts traditionally or frequently deemed 'low risk.' "

Next Cramer handed out an article by Don Durfee entitled "Management or Manipulation," CFO, December, 2006. "I have summarized his comments on this sheet."

Management or Manipulation?

- More than one-half of CFOs say they can legally influence reported earnings by 3% or more.
- Operational levers: delaying operational spending, accelerating order processing, and driving sales force more.
- Accounting steps: changing the timing of an accounting change and adjusting estimates.
- One-third of CFOs would try to influence results: 24% upward or 8% would try to cut them.
- Few CFOs think their auditors would catch them.
- If the auditors caught them, they probably would *not* bring it up to management.

"The moral of the story," Cramer emphasized, "as an auditor you must be extremely skeptical. For example, from 1999 to 2001, HealthSouth's net income increased nearly to 500%, but revenues grew only 5%. On March 19, 2003, the SEC said that HealthSouth faked at least $1.4 billion in profits since 1999 under the auditing eyes of Ernst & Young."

"The SEC said that HealthSouth started cooking its numbers in 1986, which Ernst & Young failed to find over 17 years. HealthSouth also inflated its cash balances."

Cramer wrote on the blackboard the two following entries. "These are the two entries used by HealthSouth to cook their books."

Suspense Account	XX	
Revenue		XX
Accounts Receivable	XX	
Inventory	XX	
Property	XX	
Suspense Account		XXX

"Most of the entries were inter-company entries, since Health-South used PeopleSoft, with at least 2,000 different ledgers. If you see a 'suspense account,' be careful. The assets accounts were manufactured. They did not exist."

Cramer wrote another entry on the blackboard:

Property, Plant & Equipment	$629,000,000	
Construction in Progress	142,000,000	
Operating Expenses		771,000,000

"The initial line costs at WorldCom were expensed properly early in the year. However, the CFO encouraged Betty Vinson to make several entries like I have written on the board. The backup or support for these entries were yellow post-it notes. Betty Vinson served time in prison. Do not allow a boss to talk you into cooking the books."

"Well, I see we're nearly out of time. Does anyone have any questions or comments about legal liability or anything?"

Cramer waited a moment. No one responded to his question. He then asked, "Has anyone read anything about auditing recently? In the newspaper or a professional journal?"

Everyone started stacking their books, anxious to leave the classroom. Suddenly there was a murmur of discontent as Dane Miller raised his hand. Cramer motioned for Dane to ask his question.

"Dr. Cramer, I saw an article in last month's *Journal of Accountancy* that referred to the expectations gap. What's that?" The question was asked by one of Cramer's favorite students. Jeff seemed genuinely interested in learning.

"Jeff, that is a real troublesome issue to the profession. The problem relates to the misunderstanding or misperception by the general public regarding the auditor's role in an audit."

"I get it," Jeff interrupted. "The public expects something different from what the auditor actually does."

"Exactly," Cramer responded. Cramer smiled. He had already prepared some lecture notes on this topic. He pulled out some pages from among his voluminous lecture notes and began talking again.

"The general counsel of one Big Four firm described the misperception problem several years ago. He stated that misconceptions in the public mind are at least fivefold. The first area relates to scope—that auditors make a 100% examination of the company's records, which can be depended upon to uncover all errors or misconduct. The second area relates to evaluation—that auditors evaluate the wisdom and legality of a company's multitudinous business decisions. The third area concerns precision—that the numbers set forth in a company's audited financial statements are immutable absolutes. The fourth area relates to reducibility—that the audited results of a company's operations for a year can be synthesized into a single number. The fifth area concerns approval—that by expressing an opinion on a company's financial statement, the auditors 'certify' its health and attractiveness for investment purposes."

Cramer paused a minute while his students briskly wrote notes on his remarks. When most students stopped writing, he began again.

"The public must understand that an accountant differs from a product manufacturer in several important respects. An auditor does not have absolute control over a company's finances and records in the same way that a product manufacturer has knowledge of and control over their production processes. The relationship between the auditor and the client's financial statements, which are the responsibility of management, is indirect. Whereas the relationship between a defective product and the manufacturer is direct."

"The effect of these misconceptions results in the failure of the courts and juries to distinguish between an audit failure and a business failure. Although an auditor adds credibility to financial statements through an independent examination, the extent to which the auditor's report affects the judgment of investors is uncertain and speculative. In purchasing a product, a consumer expects an adequate product. In accountant's liability litigation there seems to be a failure in understanding a basic fact that rational investors take risks hoping to reap financial profit from their investments. They, however, should be aware of the ever-present possibility of loss."

"Recent research suggests that many financial statement users misunderstand the auditor's role and responsibilities. Users may be unaware of limitations of the audit function and may be unclear regarding the distinction between the responsibilities of management and those of the auditor. There is an ongoing effort by the profession to more clearly explain these responsibilities, and thus, to close the expectations gap. In fact, in November 2007, the Big Four said in a Global Report that there was a need for a forensic audit of public companies every three or four years. They actually admitted that accountants have a hard time finding fraud in the typical audit."

Cramer noticed several students had started shuffling around in their seats. Dane was the only one who appeared to be listening with any interest.

"Well, I see you are ready to go. Class dismissed. Adios." Everyone jumped up and headed out of the classroom. Cramer thought to himself that the whole process resembled a cattle stampede. He thought that education was the only industry where the less you gave the participants, the happier they were.

Cramer went back to his office to work on an examination. Before class he had developed this test question about detection risk:

10. An auditor wishes to hold audit risk to 2 percent for a diamond inventory and estimates from evidence obtained in prior audits found that inherent risk is 50 percent and control risk is 40 percent. Calculate the acceptable level of detection risk for the diamond inventory.

    a.   4%
    b.   6%
    c.   10%
    d.   20%
    e.   Some other amount.

The correct answer was C, or 10 percent, calculated as follows:

$$DR = \frac{AR}{IR \times CR}$$

where AR = Audit risk
           DR = Detection risk
           IR = Inherent risk
           CR = Control risk

$$DR = \frac{2\%}{.50 \times .40}$$

The next question would probably be missed by many of his students. The answer, of course, was b., because entries are not source documents.

11. The following are possible source document fraud symptoms, except

    a.   Photocopies of missing documents.
    b.   Unusual entries at the end of a period.
    c.   Second endorsements.
    d.   Duplicate payments.
    e.   All are possible source document fraud symptoms.

Cramer always put an ethical question on his exams. Here was his conflict of interest question:

12. Which of these incidents was a conflict of interest under Ethics Interpretation 102-2?

    a.   In connection with a personal financial engagement, you plan to suggest that your client invest in a business in which you have a financial interest.
    b.   You have a significant financial interest, are a member of management, or are an executive in a company that is a major competitor of a client for which you perform management consulting services.
    c.   You serve on a city's board of tax appeals, which considers matters involving several of your tax clients.
    d.   You recommend or refer a client to a service bureau in which you or a partner in your firm has material financial interests.
    e.   All of the above.

Cramer hoped all of his students would mark "All of the above."

* * *

He thought about his daughter on the drive home. Becc wouldn't be there. She was spending the night with a new-found friend from school. Becc had made this arrangement after Cramer had been called as a witness for a Congressional hearing. He was taking a late evening flight from Hartsfield International Airport to Reagan National Airport in Washington, D.C., and would be out of town for just one night. He knew Becc was old enough to take care of herself when he was out of town, but he preferred her to stay with someone when he had to travel overnight.

Cramer was staying at the Hyatt Regency in Crystal City. Crystal City is a conglomeration of hotels and shops close to Reagan National Airport; consequently, a cab ride from airport to hotel was only about five minutes. Cramer preferred short cab rides, even when he wasn't exhausted after a flight.

After stopping by the house, he headed over to Hartsfield. The only luggage he had was his Dell laptop computer and a hanging bag. He carried these on the plane, and the flight was uneventful. He did enjoy the bird's eye view of the nation's capital at night. Landing at Reagan National Airport was a little discomforting. The runways at this older airport were shorter than most; consequently, the large passenger jets had to brake rather hard on landing. "The airport's convenient location is well worth this small price, though," Cramer thought.

The cab ride and hotel check-in went smoothly. Before going to sleep he looked over some information about the Dingell Committee before which he was scheduled to testify in the morning. But his mind would drift back to Don Ball and Doyle Loebbecke. "Were they the bad guys? Was it someone else?"

Chapter 12

The objectives of the auditor's review of accounting control within EDP are similar to those for manual and mechanical processing. The review is an information-gathering process that depends on knowledgeable inquiries directed to client personnel, observation of job assignments and operating procedures, and reference to available documentation related to accounting control.

—AICPA Professional Standards

"Before I introduce our next witness, let me quote from a recent article in the *Wall Street Journal* by Lee Berton." The speaker was Congressman John D. Dingell (D-Michigan), who was chairing the Subcommittee on Oversight of Investigations of the House Energy and Commerce Committee.

"Mr. Berton indicates that many investors wonder how an outside auditor can give a clean opinion to financial results that so quickly turn sour. They have long believed that a clean opinion — one not citing any severe corporate problems — is like the Good Housekeeping Seal of Approval."

Lenny Cramer was waiting to testify before Dingell's committee. He was not quite as nervous as the last time he testified here, but he knew that the colorful Dingell was preparing to hang Lenny out to dry. Oh well, that was the price of testifying before Congress.

John Dingell gestured toward Lenny behind the microphone. "We have here today Professor Leonard Cramer, a Certified Public Accountant and practitioner in Atlanta. He also teaches at Georgia State University. Dr. Cramer, why shouldn't auditors be more responsible for detecting management fraud? What disclosures should Congress force auditors to make on financial statements?"

After a short pause, Cramer said, "Thank you Chairman Dingell for this opportunity to speak to your committee today. First, let me point out the main function of a Certified Public Accountant."

Lenny paused for a moment as he looked at each of the five committee members. "A CPA's main function is to certify to the world that the financial statements as *prepared by management* fairly present the financial position, results of operations, and cash flows for the period audited. The auditor evaluates the accounting principles used and significant estimates, made by management, as well as evaluating the overall financial statement presentation."

"Professor Cramer," Representative Dingell interjected, "What about the discovery of management fraud? This committee has heard John Shank state: At the very time an auditor should be the most cynical and skeptical about a company is when his client is applying the most pressure." Dingell smiled broadly.

Cramer continued. "A clean opinion by an auditor is not a Good Housekeeping Seal of Approval. The financial statements are management's responsibility. Auditors cannot absolutely guarantee that financial statements prepared by management are free from material misstatement. As a CPA myself, I can only provide *reasonable assurances* that audited financials are free from any material misstatement."

"Professors Arens and Loebbecke in their fine auditing textbook point out the dilemma quite well. Let me quote them."

Cramer began reading from a photocopy page. "'The auditor cannot serve as the insurer or guarantor of financial statement accuracy or business health. The audit costs to society that would be required to achieve such high levels of assurance would exceed the benefits. Moreover, even with increased audit costs, well-planned frauds would not necessarily be discovered, nor errors of judgment eliminated.' End of quote."

"Carl Liggio, general counsel for pre-merger Arthur Young & Company indicates that an auditor who would catch all fraud would be too expensive—perhaps four to six times the cost of current audits, which run from several thousand dollars for small companies to more than one million for major corporations. Who will pay for such perfection?"

Lenny raised his voice. "Look, auditors are not trained to detect forgeries, nor will current audit procedures detect all conspiracies. Mr. Liggio tells the story about one auditor-negligence court battle involving fraud by the owner of the company. This owner sent his personal pilot by plane to intercept confirmation requests about cash and assets that the conscientious auditor had express-mailed to suppliers and lenders. The pilot signed off on the confirmations and sent them back to the unsuspecting auditor. How can an auditor catch something like that?"

"Just a moment, Dr. Cramer," another Representative interjected. "Our committee has examined a number of auditing problems where the auditor was not independent. There was Penn Square Bank where partners had below market loans with the bank in excess of one million dollars. Remember Beverly Hills Savings? Here an audit partner served on the audit engagement for a number of years and allowed overstatement of assets based on appraisals by a non-independent appraiser. What about David Duncan, the Arthur Andersen partner in charge of the Enron audit? Likewise, E&Y missed the fraud at HealthSouth for about 17 years. The internal auditors at WorldCom found the fraud, not the external auditors. Who can forget Bernie Madoff's $50 billion ponzi scheme?"

The gray-haired Representative stopped for a moment and picked up a sheet of paper. "Anita Raghavan in the *Wall Street Journal* said that the Arthur Andersen lead auditor, David Duncan, of Enron chose to go along with the flow, acquiesing in Enron's questionable maneuvers and basking in the glow that came with a cozy relationship with Enron. Duncan sometimes pressed the Enron position with Arthur Andersen's Professional Standards Group and appeared to sometimes be less than fully forthcoming with the group. He destroyed Arthur Andersen by shredding over a ton of documents relating to Enron."

Lenny raised his voice, "Let me remind you that the PCAOB is now in charge of creating the rules for external auditors of publicly-traded companies—a governmental agency. When Arthur Andersen's jury conviction was overturned by the Supreme Court, the charges against Duncan were withdrawn in December 2005.

But the AICPA Professional Standards indicate that an auditor must retain his integrity and objectivity in all phases of their practice and, when expressing opinions on financial statements, avoid involvement in situations that would impair the credibility of their independence. Certainly when a partner takes bribes and subverts his own firm's quality procedures in order to cover prior year's audit errors — as was the case with ESM — independence has been breached."

Lenny looked at Dingell, but he was conferring with someone behind him. "Thus, please let me summarize. For several decades auditors have used such substantive tests as reconciling, tracing, and vouching in order to verify mechanical accuracy. The computer has caused these traditional procedures to become less efficient and effective."

"Ronald L. Clark at Auburn University states it quite well. 'Today's auditors are increasingly using analytics to gather evidence on transactions and internal controls. Audit risk has not only increased, but the concept of how to address and control risk has changed. Computer fraud, always a problem, could rise to alarming levels due to the increased number of computer end-users, databases and communication networks.' End of quote."

"Sure there are things that auditors should do. The PCAOB suggest controls that prevent or detect unauthorized journal entries which can reduce the quarterly and annual cooking of the books. Restricting access to the general ledger system, requiring dual authorizations for manual entries, or performing periodic reviews of journal entries to identify unauthorized entries can reduce earnings management and balance sheet management. Let me quote from a PCAOB document:

> As part of obtaining an understanding of the financial reporting process, the auditor should consider how journal entries are recorded in the general ledger and whether the company has controls that would either prevent unauthorized journal entries from being made to the general ledger or directly to the financial statements or detect unauthorized entries. Test of controls over jour-

nal entries could be performed in connection with the testing of journal entries required by AU sec. 316.

Dingell interrupted. "Thank you, Dr. Cramer, for your opinion about the crisis of confidence in the accounting profession." Congressman Dingell stated further, "Auditors are paid by the same hands they oversee. They are not paid to blow the whistle against their clients. May we have the next witness."

At that point, Cramer wished he could say more, but his small contribution to this hearing had ended. He thought, "I hope the next witness does a better job than me defending our honorable profession from these unwarranted attacks. Why, these Congressmen are just trying to make names for themselves by inventing scapegoats for the country's problems. Heck, if they really wanted to do something good, they'd clean up their own act and balance the budget on a regular basis. Even the *New York Times* had encouraged Charles Rangel, Chairman of the House Ways & Means Committee to resign for failure to pay taxes. Treasury Secretary Timothy Geither was confirmed even though he did not pay self-employment taxes on money he earned from 2001–2004."

As he left the hearing, he realized he had a few hours to kill before he had to return to the Hyatt. "Great, I'll walk the Mall." He walked briskly from the Capitol that was at the east end of the Mall. Cramer laughed to himself as to recalled a story about some tourists who thought that the Washington, D.C. Mall was an indoor shopping mall full of stores. In actuality the Mall is a broad expanse of open land around which the most famous national monuments are situated. He walked down the Capitol steps looking toward the Washington Monument that stood about a mile and half away in the center of the Mall. Beyond that tall monument, at the west end was the Lincoln Memorial. Close to the Lincoln Memorial was the Mall's newest addition, the Vietnam Veteran's Memorial, referred to as "The Wall."

Cramer could not resist a brief visit inside the Air and Space Museum, one of the 14 museums operated by the Smithsonian Institution. "Funny," he thought, "the Smithsonian was established by funds bequeathed to the U.S. by an Englishman, James Smith-

son. Little did that guy know what a famous American institution
he would begin. Unlike Disneyland, admission is free."

Leaving the Air and Space Museum, Cramer continued down
the sidewalk alongside Jefferson Drive, passing the Smithsonian
Castle that housed the Institution's first museum. The Castle is
what comes to most people's minds when they think of the Smithsonian. Today it is primarily administrative offices.

Cramer walked up the hill on which the Washington Monument
stands. Flapping in the wind were the flags circling the monument.
He could not help the patriotic feeling that surged through him.
In some small way he hoped that he made a contribution to the
country's future welfare and prosperity. After resting a few minutes, he continued his long walk along the Mall, passing the large
reflecting pools, to the Lincoln Memorial. Inside the memorial,
even though he had seen Lincoln's statue before, he gazed with awe.
He read the words chiseled into the marble walls:

> ... Intelligence, patriotism, Christianity, and a firm re-
> liance on Him who has never yet forsaken this favored
> land are still competent to adjust in the best way all our
> present difficulty ... As was said three thousand years
> ago, so still it must be said, 'the judgments of the Lord
> are true and righteous altogether.'

"What a horrible time for our country," thought Cramer. "More
Americans were killed in the Civil War than all the other wars com-
bined. The sixteenth president had resolved not to allow the southern states to secede. Lincoln, a Christian, often looked for wisdom
and inspiration from the Bible. Reflecting on the prospects of a
broken nation, he quoted the words of Jesus, 'A house divided
against itself shall not stand.'"

From the Lincoln Memorial, Cramer walked over to the Vietnam Veteran's Memorial. "Another sad war," he thought. On an
earlier trip to Washington, he had found the names of several friends
and relatives lost during that bitter conflict. His eyes grew misty as
he reflected on the tragic deaths of those men, literally cut down in
their prime. "War is hell! General Sherman was absolutely right."
Wiping his eyes, he wondered if there would be a memorial for the

Iraqi war. Slowly he began his trek back to the Smithsonian Castle. There he would take the Metro, Washington's subway, to Crystal City where the Hyatt was located.

At the hotel he checked out and took the hotel's shuttle bus to National Airport. He was over an hour early for his flight. The flight was delayed and it was over two hours before he was on his way back to Atlanta. He was glad that Becc would be home to greet him.

After a cheerful reunion at home Cramer thought how fortunate he was to have a daughter. After settling into bed his mind drifted to the Coke audit. He realized he would not see Slam the next day. Slam, at the request of Posey, was accompanying Laura Bertone on an overseas trip to Poland. Cramer hoped the two of them would have a pleasant trip together. "Romance is in the air," he thought before drifting off to sleep. "Maybe I can find the smoking gun while he's gone. Don Ball? Doyle Loebbecke? Both? Someone else?"

The next morning at work, Cramer decided to ask Will Posey about Doyle Loebbecke.

"Sure I know him," Posey began. "He was the resident computer nut when I started working at Coke. But he retired not long after that."

"What do you know about him?" Cramer asked.

"Not much really. He seemed to be a refined, older gentleman. Extremely friendly. I had to get his help with some programming problems a few times. Unlike some computer experts I know, Loebbecke spoke plain English. Not computer jargon. He really knew his stuff. He could explain things so that anyone could understand. You know I really hate it when anyone tells me that some so-called expert knows his stuff, but just can't explain it to others. Heck, that expert doesn't know his stuff. He's just faking it!"

"Whoa, buddy. You're getting on one of your soapboxes. Let's get back to the subject. You remember, Loebbecke? Do you know what he's doing now?"

"Well, I heard that he's seeing the world. He sends a postcard back to the old gang here at Coke once in a while. We post them on the bulletin board in the coffee room. The last one is still up, some place in Pakistan. No, India, I think. He may be back home by now. Why are you so interested in Doyle? Some question about the computer system?"

"Yeah, basically that's it. I'll tell you all about it later." Cramer started leaving Posey's office.

"Hold on, Lenny. I just remembered something. When Laura Lee began work at Coke, she started in Loebbecke's department. She could probably tell you more about him."

Cramer scratched his head. "That's a big help, Will. I'll check with her when she gets back from overseas. Thanks for the info." Cramer turned and left Posey's office.

As he walked toward his office, Cramer mused over his new-found information. "This is great! If Loebbecke is the culprit, then Laura may be able to help us figure out exactly what he did. Meanwhile, I'll get the spy equipment Slam purchased and see if I can pick up any computer signals from outside Loebbecke's home. This caper is getting too interesting to wait until Slam and Laura get back."

Chapter 13

In a compilation engagement, the accountant compiles financial statements from management's unaudited and unreviewed accounts, and issues a report that provides literally no assurance. The service merely compiles financial statements in proper form, but is useful to rather small owner-managed companies that elect to outsource the preparation of financial statements rather than to employ accounting personnel internally. Specifically, a compilation report states that the accountant "has not audited or reviewed the financial statements and, accordingly, does not express an opinion or any form of assurance."

—David N. Ricchiute

After a short stop in Paris, their American Airlines flight landed at Tegel Airport with its hexagonal terminal building in Berlin. Slam Duncan and Laura Bertone collected their suitcases and rented a blue Ford. Slam had a difficult time getting Laura's large suitcases in the trunk. Soon they drove southwest toward the center of the city.

"We still have some time before dusk. I'll take you to see remnants of 'the Wall.' The best viewing spot is at Potsdamer Platz," Laura said.

Before 1989, the wall split Berlin in half. The Western half of the city was once a sealed island, surrounded by East Germany. The Wall appeared overnight on August 13, 1961, to prevent immigration from East Berlin. However, beginning in the fall of 1989, the wall was dismantled and the communist government allowed its citizens the freedom to travel. Civil unrest in East Germany and other communist countries pressured their leaders to make changes. East and West Germany were re-united in 1990. Political reform began taking place throughout Eastern Europe.

At Potsdamer Platz, Laura and Slam scrambled up a platform to look at what was once the East German zone. Pointing to a desolate spot, Laura said, "See that small mound of dirt? That's the air raid shelter where Hitler committed suicide in 1945."

"I read that at least three-and-one-half million Germans fled from the East to the West before the Wall was built in 1961. That was a big brain drain," Slam interjected. "After the wall was dismantled in 1989, some people left East Germany, but the overwhelming majority stayed in their native country with the hope that the new freedoms would remain in effect. Eventually the two countries merged."

The old wall was really two walls with a no-man's-land between the two. In the middle was the killing zone—land mines, attack dogs, and self-triggering shotguns. Occasionally, along the route, stood a watchtower with two soldiers. A bonus was paid for any person the guards stopped—dead or alive. The guards were never put on duty twice together to avoid the development of a friendship. Two friendly guards might have escaped together.

Laura laughed. "I'm impressed by the Berliners' attitude. Apparently most of the Wall was painted in this colorful graffiti."

"I agree. Let's get a picture of the Wall." Slam climbed down from the platform and walked over to the concrete demarcation line. He pretended to be climbing the symbol of oppression. A few sections of the Wall had been left as a reminder to what had been an oppressive communist regime. Two small sections are now at the George Bush library in College Station, Texas.

Laura snapped a shot of him. The Wall looked to be about twelve feet tall.

"What do you think YBIEN means?" Slam asked as he pointed to a slogan painted in red on the Wall.

"I don't know."

With Laura driving again, they passed the Brandenburg Gate, the entrance to the city. This majestic archway was once closed, since it is flush with what was the Berlin Wall. Laura pointed out the infamous Checkpoint Charlie, one of the once heavily guarded entrances into East Berlin. "They used to push wheeled mirrors under every vehicle to catch anyone clinging to the bottom."

After checking into their rooms at the hotel, Laura and Slam walked to the Victory Tower. Along the way the trees were green and the flowers were blooming. They passed a park and laughed at some punkish-dressed young people enjoying the wonderful weather.

The Victory Tower celebrates the end of the Franco-Prussian War. They climbed the 285 steps to the top-slowly. There was a great view of the entire city and the Brandenberg Bridge.

Laura and Slam enjoyed a long kiss at the top of the tower, standing next to the angel on top.

While looking toward eastern Berlin, Laura pointed and said, "Do you see that television tower? It is almost 1,200 feet high and the top has a revolving restaurant. When the sun shines on the restaurant, sometimes a cross appears on it. Berliners named the tower the Pope's Revenge." She leaned over and kissed Slam again, amidst the noise of the street traffic below.

Slam liked it. Coca-Cola's accounting problems were far removed from his mind.

Their hotel rooms were so small that Slam had to move two chairs out of Laura's room in order to make space for her enormous suitcase.

The next morning, because of jet lag, Slam awoke at 3:30 a.m. As they drove out of Berlin they stopped at the 1936 Olympics Stadium. Jesse Owens won his gold medals here. "Der Führer" really fumed when Owens triumphed over members of his "master race" four times. The lush green field was now used mostly for soccer.

By late morning, Laura and Slam reached what had been the East German border. Soon they were traveling across eastern Germany."We'll still see fewer Coke signs in this part of Germany," Laura commented. "Coke was not allowed here when it was East Germany.

Slam's mood turned solemn as he noticed the remnant of high fences left over from the pre-1989 days. Before the political changes, cars were not supposed to stop along the route. It was once a treasonable act for an East German to have an unauthorized contact with a Westerner. Before becoming too solemn, Slam decided to tease Laura.

"Why did Coke have so little success with the former East Germans. Coke still doesn't have a franchise in Russia. Isn't that an embarrassment? Arch-rival Pepsi is there."

"Old news. State-owned plants began bottling Coca-Cola in 1987. We formed a joint venture with Moscow to sell Coke products in Russia in 1992. You have been reading Pepsi propaganda. Pepsi did beat us there."

Laura paused as if thinking. "We're in China and Pepsi is behind. In China we have 34 percent of the unit case volume. In India we have 60 percent of the market and Pepsi only has 35 percent. Coke is in at least 200 countries. Four of the world's top five nonalcoholic sparking beverages are ours — Coca-Cola, Diet Coke, Sprite, and Fanta. We have 20 percent of the $580 billion market of nonalcoholic ready-to-drink beverages. Coke is one of the world's most popular and best recognized consumer products with 1.5 billion servings per day. More than 70 percent of Coca-Cola's net operating revenue is generated outside of the U.S." Laura protested.

"I believe Pepsi made some blunders with their advertising in China," Slam asked.

"So true. Their slogan 'Be sociable' equals 'Be intimate.' Their slogan 'Now it's Pepsi for those who think young' meant 'New Pepsi is for people with the minds of children.' Of course, our slogan 'the pause that refreshes' means 'stop and rejuvenate.' When we first went into China some of the early signs for Coke said 'Bite the Wax Tadpole.'"

Slam could tell that Laura was getting angry, so he changed the subject. "What are you going to do in Warsaw?"

"The name of the game is consolidation of resources. By consolidating plants, distribution systems, sales forces, and accounting systems — we can exploit economies of scale. We need to build a 'super plant' in order to spread our costs over the largest feasible number of Cokes."

"I have a meeting with the President of Poland tomorrow to discuss placing a super bottling plant in Poland. As you may know, Poland has the highest birth rate in Europe. I read in some underground literature that reproduction in Poland is an undercover activity." Laura laughed and said, "Maybe it was a Solidarity slogan."

"Where will it be located?" asked Slam.

"Hopefully east of Krakow, near a small town called Oswiecim. It's almost in the center of Europe with railroad tracks leading like spokes throughout Europe."

"Oswiecim. Have I heard that name before?"

"Possibly," Laura nodded. "That's where the Nazis' concentration camp Auschwitz was located. Between 1940 and 1945 more than four million, mainly Jewish, prisoners were gassed or shot by the Nazis and then burned. Of course, you can recognize our public relations problem. We'll have to create another small town near Auschwitz to avoid a possible public outcry. But Hitler selected Oswiecim because of its central location."

"Isn't there an alternate location?" Slam asked.

"Yes. Near Czestochowa. That's the location of a Pauline monastery which houses the holiest shrine in the country—the Black Madonna. Of course, Oswiecim is the best location. Our super plant must be on rail spurs in order to reduce shipping costs."

"Some dilemma," said Slam. "Should Coke pick the best location at the site of the most appalling inhumanity to mankind or pick the lesser location at the center of religious and cultural life of Poland? What spot would the Pope pick?"

"Hey, just south of Oswiecim is Wadowice, the birthplace of Pope John Paul II," smiled Laura.

"Just why are you here?" asked Slam. "You're a computer whiz, not a marketing expert."

"The production facility will be controlled by a black box data processing system. The big computer will run eight to ten lines at high speed. We are talking about 1,600 to 2,000 containers per minute."

"What did Churchill say? Never has so much been delivered to so many by so few." After a few moments Slam continued. "I thought there was an embargo of high-tech computers to former communist countries."

"Very perceptive!" responded Laura. "That's why Lech Walesa is helping us tomorrow. He's the same person who negotiated the political agreement for Solidarity in 1989. Lech Walesa won the Nobel Peace Prize in 1983, and he served as President of Poland from

1990 until 1995. He's into IT now. We must negotiate some type of business agreement to assure the State Department that the big computer will not get into the hands of their military. "

At Frankfurt-an-der-Oder they crossed the Oder River to go to Poland. They stopped and a Polish border guard checked their passports and visas. They filled out a declaration form indicating how much money they were carrying into Poland. Any excess currency of what is entered on the form is subject to confiscation. Also, travelers to Poland must exchange a minimum of $15 per day at the official exchange rate.

Poland is slightly smaller than New Mexico, and after almost 50 years of Soviet-enforced Marxism-Leninism, is one of the poorest of the Eastern bloc countries. Unstable, with a steadily deteriorating quality of life, its 38.5 million inhabitants live a grim daily existence. Although Communist-ruled for many years, its citizens are devoutly religious and about 85 percent of the land is privately owned. The Catholic Church is an important force with more than 90 percent of the people Roman Catholics. Even communist oppression could not eradicate Christianity. For that matter, neither could Roman oppression two thousand years earlier.

The road across the flat terrain was in poor condition, and when Laura and Slam turned onto a minor road to a small town named Rzepin, it was narrow, with some horse-drawn carts. They had noticed some carts being used in the fields, and some landowners using sickles to cut their crops.

Rzepin was a little town with about 15,000 people. The quaint, little restaurant served an enjoyable lunch. They started with an appetizer of baked chicken, followed with a bowl of potato soup with mushrooms, a cucumber salad, and sliced tomato. Then came the pork chops, with gravy, potatoes, custard, Coke, and vodka.

"Some lunch," said Slam outside the restaurant.

"You understand, Slam, that food supplies are still somewhat erratic in Poland," Laura said. "A housewife might spend some time each day in a line trying to buy food for her family."

Laura saw a little girl sitting on the steps next door to the restaurant. She took her picture, and then gave her a 50 Zoltys coin. The little girl beamed.

Since Warsaw was about 320 miles from the German border, it was about 7:30 when they arrived at the Novotel Warszawa Centrum in Warsaw, the capital of Poland. After getting their luggage to their rooms, they took a cab to the Old Market restaurant called Kamienne Schodki. Tucked away at the corner of the Old Market, stone stairs descend to the Vistula River that bisects Warsaw.

While waiting for their roast duck, Laura gave Slam a short history of Warsaw. "Poland was the first country attacked by Nazi Germany in 1939. No other city suffered more than Warsaw during the war. Hitler gave orders to destroy Warsaw. There were four weeks of bombing, and then the German soldiers completely razed the city to the ground. Nothing was left in the systematic destruction, except 45,000 corpses under the ruins. Everything, with clinical precision, was destroyed, street-by-street with dynamite and petrol. When the army of liberation entered Warsaw in January 1945, not a single human being was alive. Even Hiroshima had some survivors. What had taken 700 years to build, the Germans wiped out in less than two months."

"Like a phoenix rising from its ashes," Laura continued, "the Polish people rebuilt the city. This Old Town district was rebuilt exactly as it was before the destruction. The architects used paintings, old prints, and family photographs to rebuild 18th century buildings in this area. You noticed that Old Town is closed to all traffic except horse-drawn cabs."

"Poland is flat, but those large hills we saw as we entered Warsaw are large mounds of the debris carried from the destroyed city. Every citizen became a builder, and a new city came back to life. The bill for the tasty roast duck was 60 PLN or about $20."

While waiting on change Laura told Slam about her father's visit to Poland in the early nineties. "There was hyperinflation during the early nineties. In January 1995, the 10,000 old zloty (PLZ) became only one zloty (PLN)."

"That's super-inflation," Slam said. "I bet there were quite a few millionaires in Poland before 1995. We'll probably have super-inflation in the U.S. as a result of the huge stimulus packages in late 2008 and 2009."

* * *

The next two days for Laura involved a number of meetings with Coca-Cola's employees, Polish governmental officials, and various consultants. The discussions centered around these obstacles:

1. Pros and cons of the two plant locations — Oswiecim or Czestochowa.
2. Ways for Coca-Cola to remove any profits from Poland.
3. The percentage ownership of the participants, Coca-Cola and Poland, in the joint venture.
4. The amount each participant will provide the joint venture.
5. The control of the "super computer" by Coca-Cola in order to convince U.S. officials to allow such a powerful computer in a former communist country.

At the end of the second day the Polish government and Coca-Cola issued the following agreement that appeared in *Polityka*, a weekly journal:

> Coca-Cola and Poland have reached a tentative agreement to build a "super" bottling plant in Poland. The location of the plant is still under consideration. Coca-Cola, with a 51 percent stake, will control the joint venture. A state-of-the-art data processing system will control nine lines at high speeds, to produce 1,800 containers per minute. The profit distributable by the joint venture shall be the excess of its net profit over income tax payable and the required provisions of reserve fund, staff and workers' bonus and welfare fund and enterprise expansion fund. It shall be distributed to the participants of the joint venture in proportion to their shares of contributed capital.
>
> Each participant of the joint venture may audit the accounts of the joint venture. The expenses thereon shall be paid by the participant making the audit. Any problem noted in the audit that needs to be resolved by the joint venture shall be submitted to the joint venture in a timely manner for discussion and resolution.

The assets of the joint venture left over after the clear-
ance of all its debts shall be distributed among the participants of the joint venture according to the proportion
of each participant's investment contribution, unless
otherwise provided by the agreement, contract or articles of association of the joint venture.

Slam did not attend the two days of meetings but instead checked
on the sales account of the major Polish Coca-Cola bottler. He
knew that computer data was not a panacea for old-fashioned fact
checking. On the first morning of his audit he told Laura, "Look,
information from a computer data bank is only as good as the person who typed in the original information."

"On one U.S. audit I noticed unexplainable swings in sales transactions reported in certain branches. I finally traced the discrepancies to a clerk in Cleveland who occasionally added four zeros to
actual figures to ease boredom."

At the bottler's headquarters, Slam found that two clerks verified the quantity, price, and extension of each sale. They then ini-
tialed the duplicate invoice to indicate performance. This procedure
was a form of internal control. Thus, Slam first performed a compliance audit procedure. He examined a sample of the duplicate
sales invoices for the initials of the two women who verified the
quantitative data.

Slam found that there were a number of documents without a
signature. Thus, he had to follow-up with substantive tests. He extended his tests of the duplicate sales invoices by verifying prices,
extensions, and footings. In effect, he did a substantive test of the
transactions. He found that the invoices were correct, because the
original clerks preparing the sales invoices had done competent jobs.

Later that evening Slam told Laura that the sales figures for the
Polish branch of Coca-Cola were probably correct.

Laura related to Slam the events of her day, and they arranged
to meet for breakfast at 7 a.m. Laura wanted to visit the two alternate locations for the future bottling plant.

Chapter 14

Throughout the usual work of accountants, there is the constant pressure to follow the principles of GAAP. Audit procedures are prescribed and due adherence to the rules will produce statements of historical results and current fiscal condition, which meet all the criteria.

— Melvin I. Shapiro, CPA

As they were leaving Warsaw early Wednesday morning, Laura asked Slam, "Do you know the best spot to view Warsaw?"

Without waiting for a response Laura pointed to a tall building. "The best vantage point from which to admire Warsaw is from atop the 42-story Palace of Culture and Science. It's a wedding-cake-skyscraper gift from Stalin in 1955, and one of the taller buildings in Poland. That's one of the spots in the city from which you can avoid looking at the ugly Stalin-Gothic style."

"I like it," Slam said. "The Wedding Cake building."

"You would," Laura laughed. "The 778-foot landmark houses museums, theaters, libraries, swimming pools, restaurants, and the Academy of Science. It's the cultural center of Warsaw. We may get to hear a Chopin recital. Chopin was born just outside Warsaw."

Laura negotiated the blue Ford south. She pointed out the fine stucco facades of the 19th century houses. "They are not hidden by commercial signs yet," Laura commented. After leaving Warsaw, she took E82, through Tomaszow Maz and Piotrkow Tryb, toward Czestochowa.

Slam asked, "I've seen a lot of flower peddlers in Warsaw. What's the holiday?"

"No holiday," Laura replied, "There's an age-old Polish tradition of giving flowers on almost any occasion. There are many wealthy farmers who grow roses in glass-covered hothouses."

Some horses pulled people in rickety wooden carts along the shoulder of the two-lane road. Farmers pitched hay onto wagons in the fields. There were small fields of barley, wheat, cabbage, and potatoes. Slam noticed the single, box-shaped farmhouses on both sides of the road. Even the huts, however, had a TV antenna on top to watch the two nation-wide channels or 12 regional channels. There are more than ten million television sets in Poland—one for every four people. There are VCRs, also. Every few miles Slam saw a cross or a shrine with a figure of the Madonna or Christ, with fresh-cut flowers.

Laura was driving behind a Polish-built Polonez auto as they entered the small town of Czestochowa, the home of the holiest shrine in Poland. "I'm supposed to meet someone at the Dom Pielgrzyma, which is adjacent to the Jasna Gora complex. We're a little early, so let's go to the coffee shop there," she said.

The service was slow, but Laura pulled out an old brochure and started telling Slam about the famous place of pilgrimage for the Poles.

"The object of so many walking pilgrims is Our Lady of Czestochowa, better known as the Black Madonna—not the rock singer in the states. Legend attributes the icon to St. Luke the Evangelist. By the way, Jasna Gora means 'Bright Hill.'"

Laura pointed to the photo in the brochure. "The painting shows Madonna with the Christ child on her left arm. The child is holding a book, known as a Hogegetria. The Poles credit the painting for saving their country in 1655. 'Our Lady' gave 230 defenders the strength to repel 4,000 Protestant Swedish invaders. The Jasna Gora basilica is Poland's only unconquered fortification."

"What are the two long marks on her right cheek?" Slam asked.

"Again legend states that the scars on her face were inflicted by a would-be Tartar thief who struck it twice with his sword. While preparing to strike it again, he apparently then fell dead."

Pointing to the photo Slam inquired again, "Why are their faces dark?"

"The original painting may have been from the Fifth century. Thus, some scholars believe it is an exact image of the Virgin Mary.

She was a young Jewish woman from Palestine, and people from that region were dark."

"Bear in mind," Laura continued, "that the four feet by three feet icon was really completely repainted in 1434 on three repaired cyprus planks from the top of the table of the Holy Family in Nazareth. A woven canvas was glued to the boards and the artists copied the original damaged painting."

Slam read the short description of the painting by the historian Canon Jan Dlugosz of Kracow:

"A picture of Mary, the most glorious and the most venerable virgin, the queen of the world and of the Poles, which has been executed with a strange and extraordinary skill, with a serene expression on Her face from whatever direction you look at it. Looking at this picture one is pervaded with a sense of peculiar piety, as if looking at a living person."

"Martin! We are over here." Laura stood up and motioned to a thin, dark-headed person entering the door. When Martin reached the table, Laura shook his hand and said, "Martin Wojdak, I wish you to meet Slam Duncan. Have a seat?" Martin was wearing a Coca-Cola uniform, with an open-neck shirt.

"I can't stay long. I still have some more deliveries to make," Martin replied in heavily accented English.

Laura spoke to Slam. "Martin is probably the only Protestant living in Poland. His great-grandfather was one of the 4,000 Swedish invaders who were repelled by the Poles at Jasna Gora basilica."

"Come on, Laura; don't make up stories. You'll get me in trouble," Martin responded cautiously.

"Don't worry about Slam. How's your son? He's about 13 now, right?"

"Jerzy is only 12. Still thin and tall for his age. My whole family is doing fine." Martin appeared nervous to Slam.

Looking at Slam, Laura said, "Martin drives a Coke truck in this area. He also repairs machinery on the side." Turning back to Martin she asked, "Do you still have to sign a list every morning for two months in order to buy a washing machine in Poland?"

Martin broke his first smile and said, "No longer, but a businessman still has many headaches in Poland. I have arranged for you to take a tour of Jasna Gora with a priest who spent some time in the U.S.A. He's going to guide some American tourists at 1:15. Let us walk over and meet him." Martin rose.

Slam took a last sip from his cup of tea, went to pay the bill, but he overheard Laura ask Martin, "Are they in place?"

"Yes, for about four months," was Martin's response in a whisper.

At the monastery Laura and Slam joined a tour group of Americans, most of them accounting students and professors from Texas. They met Fr. Simon Ratynski in the courtyard with the greyish coat-of-arms of the Paulite Order designed into the dirty-white cobblestone. One accounting professor asked Simon, "What type of accounting system does the church use?"

Simon responded smiling, "I'm just a priest." After walking through the Lubomirski Gate, Simon, who spoke excellent English, led the group into the Chapel of Our Lady, through a front door. He took the group of eighteen into the front of the Chapel while a service was proceeding. The Chapel was filled with worshipers singing "Ave Maria." Slam noticed, as he entered, the Baroque stucco decorations in the main part of the interior of the church. There were four side altars and three portals of black marble. The vaulted ceilings were adorned with stucco patterns.

The ebony High Altar contains the Miraculous Picture, surrounded by silver angel ornaments. Above the altar was a pitched canopy of cloth. Slam tried to tiptoe on the black-and-white-marble floor as he moved to get a closer look at the Black Madonna. No photos were allowed.

Slam was able to see the coloration of the Madonna's face with the two scars. The Madonna and Child wore a gown, which was an elaborate overlay of gem-encrusted gold and silver. Before they had entered, Simon indicated that the golden crowns over the heads of the Madonna and child were presented by Pope Pius X in 1910 in connection with the coronation of the icon.

After leaving the Chapel, Simon took the group to a large room with many gifts received by the Paulite Order. Simon merely took a key pinned to his robe and unlocked the wooden door to the room. Slam noticed a simple alarm system attached to the door. There were thousands and thousands of gold and silver items, diamonds, rubies and other precious stones in the glass-encased storage cases. Many wedding and diamond rings, brooches, old coins, tie tacs, and other ornaments were displayed in the large room.

Next Simon took the group to another room where most members bought some souvenirs. Simon was quite a character and an excellent salesperson. Laura bought a Coke from a bright red Coca-Cola machine, and seemed quite pleased. Outside many of the tour members gave Simon a tip, which he readily accepted. One professor got him to pose giving the Aggie sign, an uplifted thumb with clinched fingers. What a sight in Poland: a Polish priest posing with a "good bull" fighting symbol. Shades of Solidarity.

Once Laura and Slam started driving toward Oswiecim, Slam began flipping through the book Laura had bought: *Shrine of the Black Madonna at Czestochowa,* by Janusz St. Pasierb.

Almost talking to himself Slam said, "This place has a collection of armour and firearms, musical instruments, portraits, old books and records—Wow! Listen to this. There's a huge gold monstrance. What's a monstrance?"

"That's a vessel in which the consecrated Host is exposed for the veneration of the faithful," Laura spoke calmly.

"Anyway, there's two cloisonné high priests, Melchizedek and Aaron, holding their hands pointing to the Host. The crown has a large diamond, plus 2,366 diamonds, 2,208 rubies, 214 pearls, 81 emeralds, and 30 sapphires." Slam rubbed his finger tips over the glossy picture of the crown in the book.

Slam read for a time while Laura drove in silence. Finally he asked, "Did you know that there are five different robes for the Black Madonna? A ruby robe, a diamond robe—"

"What are the other three robes?" Laura asked quietly.

"I don't know. Can't find it in this book." Slam closed the book with a bang. "I should have bought one of these books."

* * *

Their next stop was the Auschwitz concentration camp near Oswiecim. The words on the gate say: Work Brings Freedom. Yet the only way out for four-and-one half years was "through the chimney." The camp has been left as it was found by the Soviets on

January 27, 1945 as a grim reminder. From the watchtower at the entrance, Slam and Laura saw the enormity of the largest Nazi death camp. The barracks and crematoria are now museums of the Nazi atrocities, where four million people from 29 nationalities were brought to die after being told they were moving to re-settlement areas.

As the people debarked from their train, an S.S. physician determined the fate of the prisoners with either of two words—right or left. About 75 percent of the people were directed straight into the gas chambers—after they removed their clothes. The exhibits showed how progressively efficient the Nazis became. Shooting was too slow, so they built a gas chamber. Slam shivered as he imagined an S.S. efficiency expert moving through the camp making observations and calculations.

There was a huge bin of 5,000 children's shoes, a large bin of false legs, a bin of hair—all being saved by the Nazis to be sent back to the front lines. Gold was removed from corpses' teeth after the gas chamber. The horrible sights and photos of lamps made of skin gave Slam a strange experience of mixed feelings. One exhibit indicated that twins were especially important for the human experiments performed by the S.S. doctors at the camp.

Later outside Laura asked Slam, "Well, can we locate the plant site here?"

Slam breathed slowly and responded, "Ask me tomorrow."

After a short drive to Kracow, the ancient seat of the Polish Kings, Laura and Slam stopped at Orbis-Holiday Inn for the night. Laura spent much of the evening sorting through notes involving the installation of the super computer. Slam noticed that she had Coca-Cola's Accounting Manual open to the section on security over automatic systems.

Slam watched a Polish version of "Grease" on the television as he read a paperback novel. At one point Laura looked up and Slam asked, "Are you a member of the Institute of Internal Auditors?"

"Sure," was Laura's swift response. "I'm a CIA—Certified Internal Auditor. We have standards of Professional Practice like CPAs. Why do you ask?"

"Oh, no reason," Slam responded impassively. "What are you reading?" Laura asked.

"Oh, a book by Dick Francis called Risk. Here, read these two paragraphs." Laura read out loud:

"Although the majority of mankind think of auditing accountants as dry-as-dust creatures burrowing dimly into columns of boring figures, the dishonest regard them as deadly enemies."

"I have had my share of uncovering frauds. I'd lost a dozen people their jobs and set the Revenue onto others, and seen five embezzlers go to prison, and the spite in some of those eyes had been like acid."

Laura then asked, "English accountant? Right?" Slam nodded.

After Slam retired to his room for the evening, Laura continued working on her computer late into the night. She discovered that some of the files she needed were not on her flash drive, so she used the modem on her laptop to connect via phone line to her computer in Atlanta.

The next morning they drove to the small town of Wieliczka, about eight miles southeast of Kracow, in the sub-Carpathian foothills. Wieliczka has one of the biggest and oldest salt mines in Europe, producing about 700 tons of pure salt a day.

Laura and Slam elected to take an old elevator down the Danilowicz shaft, rather than the 394 step walk. An English-speaking guide met them and six other Americans at the start of the tourist route.

The Polish guide spoke very loudly, "Hello, I am a former salt miner, and I will be your guide for the next two hours! No smoking. Watch your head. Do not touch electric fittings. This salt mine has been in existence for 700 years. There are 20 chambers open to the public along a one-and-a-half mile route. We will descend through three levels to a depth of 442 feet."

"For a long time the sea covered this area, but gradually the sea water evaporated, leaving behind a large quantity of salt. Beams and huge logs reinforce the caves and stalls. Over the centuries this mine has swallowed vast forests, but fortunately, wood does not rot in a salt-mine. The wood becomes saturated with salt and can last for centuries."

"Miners do not merely dig salt, but some pious miners knew how to carve with salt. Among the carvings you will see today are eight salt gnomes, Holy Cross chapel, methane burners, St. Anton's chapel, Nicolos Copernicus, Princess Kinga, Joseph and Mary with baby Jesus, and a legendary ghost who guards this underground salt-treasure. Follow me and stay close."

The walk underground was fantastic. Along the way in the various chambers and stalls were beautiful statues and reliefs hewed out of the greyish rock salt. The lighting in the subterranean caves made some of the artwork bright white. Periodically along the way Slam would give Laura a short kiss or put his arm around her. She never protested.

At the underground snack bar most of the group members rested on the wooden benches. At this time the guide told a tall tale about meeting a woman from Chicago. "She has invited me to come visit her in Chicago, so I will gladly accept American dollars as tips."

Laura whispered to Slam. "Do you think he is conning us? They really like hard currency."

After eating ice cream bars and posting some postcards in the underground post office, Laura and Slam continued the tour. The most impressive chamber in the mine was the 180-feet long Chapel of St. Kinga with octagon-shaped stone flooring. There was a delicate seventeenth-century salt altar, illuminated by five salt chandeliers. Lovely salt statues and bas-reliefs surround the chapel, with a salt version of the Last Supper.

On a lower level were two chambers with two lakes leading to Stanislaw Staszic stall. With a height of 137 feet, the Nazis installed a plant to produce motors for their aircraft during World War II in this chamber. Jewish workers, not miners, were used in this part of the mine. Before the arrival of the Soviet army, the workers were sent to Auschwitz.

After the salt mine tour, Laura and Slam drove back toward Warsaw on E7, passing through Kielce and Radom, to Okecie Airport, about six miles south of Warsaw. Slam had been unexpectedly called back to Atlanta by Cramer. Apparently, Cramer needed some help with an unexpected computer-related problem. Laura planned to travel to Finland and Moscow for a week. They said goodbye at the airport. Slam caught a flight to Frankfurt, connecting with a United Airlines direct flight to Atlanta.

Chapter 15

The worst moment on the worst day of [Walter] Pavlo's life came on March 14, 2001 when he kissed Rhoda, Bubby, and Howie goodbye and headed out the door for the ride to prison. His younger brother Chris was waiting in the driveway. Their destination was the federal prison in Jesup, Georgia, two hours south of Savannah. Walter Pavlo, Jr.

—Neil Weinberg

Cramer was deeply troubled. Some very disturbing findings from his audit investigation had required that he call Slam home from his European travels with Laura. At the moment, however, he simply had to forget his personal concerns and concentrate on his lecture. He looked across the classroom, mentally noting the pre-class activities of his students. Many were talking, some were reading the campus newspaper, and a few were even studying.

He began his lecture. "Today we will examine a critical area of accounting practice; that is, how to effectively research accounting and auditing problems." Most of the students began taking notes.

"The increasingly complex environment facing professional accountants, whether in public practice, industry, or government, often presents problems requiring the in-depth consideration of numerous and complex accounting and auditing issues."

"Accounting and auditing issues are becoming more complex and problems requiring research are being encountered with increasing frequency. While researching tax problems is a normal procedure for many, if not most, practicing accountants, the process of researching accounting and auditing problems is much less familiar."

"The purpose of my lecture is as follows: one, define research; two, discuss the research process; and three, discuss research reference sources; all from the viewpoint of the practicing accountant. David Aaker and George Day state that 'there are always pivotal questions in the research process. How crucial is the decision? If the wrong decision is made, what will the consequences be?'"

"Research enhances and strengthens the accountant's overall competence and efficiency by enabling an accountant to identify the authoritative, technical information on which sound judgment is based. Research strengthens the accountant's credibility. Research allows an accountant to match the applicable authoritative pronouncements to the accounting and auditing problems encountered."

"In addition to tax, accounting, and auditing services, research is particularly beneficial to the accountant in management consulting engagements. For example, accounting research may be used to identify methods of improving a client's cash flow. It helps the accountant analyze the financial implications of major changes in the client's business operations. Research keeps the accountant, and thus the accountant's clients, up to date on accounting developments and their impact on financial reporting."

"While research is frequently done by accountants in government and industry, accounting and auditing research is especially useful to accountants in public practice. Because of the sheer number and varied backgrounds of their clients, public accounting firms are continually conducting research dealing with a diversity of accounting and auditing issues. The time and resources devoted to research by a number of the larger multi-office firms have led them to establish separate research departments to provide support to the accountants in their everyday work on engagements."

"Research, in general, is an objective, formal process for systematically obtaining, analyzing, and interpreting data for the purpose of providing information useful for decision making. Research may be categorized as pure or applied."

"Pure or basic research may have little or no practical application. Pure accounting research includes the development and testing of new theories of 'how the world works' with respect to accounting practices. Examples of questions asked might include:

one, does the manner in which we as a practice, or as a profession, account for transactions and events make a difference? Or two, does our audit examination and report on the condition of the client's operations make a difference? This type of research, which has little immediate practical application, is often in the form of empirical research, that is, research based on an experiment or observation. Pure research is done more by academics, that is, professors, rather than by practitioners."

"Applied or practical research, the primary subject matter of this lecture, deals with the analysis of a particular question or problem of immediate practical concern. For example, a client may be considering the acquisition of new plant equipment and may wish to know the effects this acquisition will have on the financial statements. If the client seeks the accountant's advice before the transaction occurs, then the accountant conducts a priori, before the fact, research. Research regarding a completed transaction is referred to as a posterior, after the fact."

"For the practitioner, applied or practical research may be described as a logical process of acquiring and documenting evidence supporting a conclusion regarding an accounting or auditing issue or problem. Properly documenting the research process is a basic and essential characteristic of good research."

"Both pure and applied research is essential to the accounting profession. Applied research is obviously necessary to solve the practical problems encountered in everyday practice. It is related to the technical competence the business community expects from the accounting profession. Pure research contributes to the overall body of accounting knowledge and, hopefully, will eventually be of assistance in solving practical problems."

A student's hand being raised captured Lenny's attention. "Yes," he responded. "What's your question, Randy?"

Randy usually asked thoughtful questions that were not easily answered. Cramer enjoyed interacting with all of his students, but he particularly appreciated feedback from students like Randy.

"Is this a 'publish or perish' school, Dr. Cramer?" Without waiting for a response, Randy continued, "Do you like teaching or research the most?" Many of the students looked up from their note taking.

Although Cramer was a little surprised by the personal nature of Randy's inquiries, he tried to look impassive as he replied. "Those are two good questions, Randy. My lecture, as I've previously indicated, is chiefly concerned with practitioner research, rather than a professor's research. Thus, your questions are a little off the subject. However, I will answer them anyway." A few students chuckled.

"Regarding your first question, virtually all schools expect some research activity from their faculties. I believe research is important because it helps professors stay up-to-date and enthusiastic about recent developments in the accounting field. Consequently, professors can do a better job teaching by being involved in some research. Regarding your second question, I always give my students' problems priority over my research projects. I consider teaching and counseling students more important than research, but as I've indicated, some research is necessary."

Cramer paused. He asked, "Does anyone else have a question?" When no one responded, he resumed his lecture.

"The fundamental steps in the research process include the following: problem identification, planning the research, gathering evidence, evaluating evidence, and drawing a conclusion. Problem identification is the initial step in the research process. For example, a client may ask the accountant to determine the impact of a particular transaction. Usually, further refinement of the precise problem is necessary. The practitioner must identify the problem as specifically as possible, to avoid wasting time and effort reviewing sources which are not relevant to the specific issues under consideration. The starting point for effective research is a clear identification of the problem."

For example, if you have to audit the production of a movie, you have to research and learn about it. Production accounting is a specialized form of project accounting that tracks the cost of an individual movie or television episode film production costs. A movie or television studio hires a production accountant to keep track of the costs of the movie or episode.

"The second step in the research process is planning a specific strategy for carrying out and completing the research. Three components are included in planning the research project. The first is an overview of the accounting or auditing problem under consideration. This overview includes a statement of the research objectives and research questions to be answered. Second, the research methodology is identified as one, data to be collected; two, procedures to be used in collecting the data; and, three, techniques to be used in analyzing the data. Finally, the researcher's resources, principally time, are allocated and scheduled."

"Once the problem is clearly identified and a research plan is developed, the practitioner is ready to gather the appropriate evidence. This step typically includes a detailed review of relevant authoritative accounting or auditing literature, as well as a survey of current practice. The primary sources of authoritative accounting literature are shown here:"

Cramer paused to place a sheet on the Elmo projector. The projector displayed the following information.

Highest level of accounting authority:

1. Non-superseded sections of the Accounting Research Bulletins issued by the Committee on Accounting Procedures.
2. Non-superseded sections of the APB Opinions issued by the Accounting Principles Board.
3. Statements of Financial Accounting Standards issued by the FASB.
4. Interpretations issued by the FASB.
5. Statements and Interpretations of the Governmental Accounting Standards Board (for governmental units).
6. Statements and releases of the Public Company Accounting Oversight Board.

Next level of accounting authority:

1. AICPA Industry Accounting Guides.
2. AICPA Statements of Position.
3. FASB and GASB Technical Bulletins.
4. Industry accounting practices.
5. AICPA Accounting Interpretations.

Lower level of accounting authority:

1. Guidelines published by PCAOB, SEC, and other regulatory agencies.
2. FASB and GASB Concept Statements.
3. APB Statements.
4. AICPA Issues Papers.
5. Minutes of the FASB Emerging Issues Task Force.
6. Other professional association statements (e.g., IIA).
7. Accounting textbooks, reference books, and articles written by recognized authorities in the field.

"The literature with the highest level of accounting authority is designated by Rule 203 of the AICPA *Code of Professional Ethics* as 'accounting principles promulgated by the body designated by Council to establish such principles.' The FASB is the source presently designated to promulgate accounting principles. If a transaction or event is not covered under Rule 203, then AU Section 411 provides further guidance in determining the acceptable accounting treatment."

"Back to my movie example. The GAAP rules for film companies are found in AICPA Statement of Position 00-2 — called SOP 00-2. These are the rules used for calculating the earnings of a film company to be reported to the SEC, shareholders, and lenders. Prior to 2001, film companies had to follow Financial Accounting Standards No. 53, which required many types of costs to be capitalized. How many of you have worked on a movie?"

No one raised their hands. "One of the first audits I had to work on was MGM in New York City. Metro Goldwym Mayer made such movies as Valkyrie, Quantum of Solace, Platoon, Rain Man, and Dances with Wolves."

"Auditing, on the other hand, is a different process than accounting. Auditing may be defined as follows: 'a systematic process of objectively obtaining and evaluating evidence regarding assertions about economic actions and events to ascertain the degree of correspondence between those assertions and established criteria and communicating the results to interested users.'"

"Auditing, the attest function, aids users of accounting information by evaluating the quality of the information presented. Auditing considers business events and conditions, but does not encompass the tasks of measuring or communicating accounting issues for propriety. Auditing is primarily analytical, rather than constructive. It is investigative in nature. I believe in order to be a good auditor, you must be a good detective. Auditing concerns proof, the basis for financial statements. Auditing concepts and methodology are founded less on accounting principles, and more on the general principle of logic. I encourage you to read detective novels. How many of you read novels?" A few hands went up. "Watch detective and legal-type movies?"

"The fourth major step in the research process consists of evaluating evidence gathered from the authoritative literature and identifying alternative actions. During this process, tentative conclusions may be drawn. If alternative actions are not supported by precise rules found in the authoritative literature, then actions should be theoretically justified. One may need to conduct additional research regarding alternative actions. This research may include consultation with colleagues, as well as further discussions with the client. Naturally, the researcher must remain objective throughout the process and keep in mind that the client may be biased."

"Following the detailed analysis of each alternative action, the CPA arrives at a logical conclusion. This conclusion should be well documented and based on the evidence gathered. The conclusion is ultimately presented to the client as the proposed solution to the problem."

A student sitting near the back of the classroom did not raise her hand, but asked, "What if the client doesn't like the auditor's solution?"

"That's a dilemma," Cramer replied. "If they can't resolve their differences, then the auditor may have to withdraw from the engagement. One red flag of financial statement fraud is frequent changes in the auditor."

Cramer resumed his lecture. "In deriving the conclusion, an accountant or auditor frequently employs his or her professional judgment. Opinions of other professionals also may be consulted. Several published and online sources enable the practitioner to determine

how others have dealt with particular accounting and reporting issues."

"One useful source is *Technical Practice Aids*, which is published
by the AICPA. This service includes inquiries and responses de-
scribing actual problems encountered in practice. The response includes the interpretation and recommendations, as well as the
relevant standards and authoritative sources."

"Another useful source is *Accounting Trends & Techniques* which
is published annually by the AICPA. It illustrates current reporting
practices."

"A third is *National Automated Accounting Research System*, or
simply NAARS, which is maintained by the AICPA. NAARS is full
text, online. It includes the annual reports of over 4,200 publicly-
held corporations."

"Staying up-to-date regarding generally accepted accounting
principles (GAAP) and PCAOB directions can be challenging. Rule
203 of the American Institute of CPAs Code of Professional Conduct specifies the organizations that establish GAAP. These include
the Financial Accounting Standards Board (FASB) for private business firms; the Governmental Accounting Standards Board (GASB)
for state and local governmental entities; and the Federal Accounting
Standards Advisory Board (FASAB) for federal government entities. For each of these organizations, the highest level of GAAP is
called Category A, second highest is Category B, etc. For example,
regarding FASB, Category A GAAP are the FASB Statements of Financial Accounting Standards, together with Accounting Research
Bulletins and Accounting Principles Board Opinions which are not
superseded by action of the FASB."

"The Financial Accounting Standards Board website
(www.fasb.org) is helpful for following the FASB and Emerging Issues Task Force (EITF) activities. The Publications section contains
summaries of all FASB Statements (Category A GAAP). These online summaries are the same as those inside the printed standards.
The Emerging Issues Task Force section, found under the Technical Projects link, provides a summary of current issues the EITF
has discussed and indicates if a consensus was reached. EITF consensus positions are Category C GAAP. This link also provides ac-

cess to the Technical Inquiry Service. This section contains an on-line form that allows you to submit questions about FASB literature and projects. The site provides a wealth of information about the FASB's and EITF's projects. These include meeting agendas, exposure drafts, press releases, a quarterly plan of technical items under review, and e-mail addresses for contacting the FASB board members and staff."

"The Public Company Accounting Oversight Board website (www.pcaob.com) provides information about the PCAOB activities. The Public Company Accounting Oversight Board performs annual peer reviews of audit firms with 100 or more public company audit clients and every three years for all other firms with public company audit clients. The Board has the authority to investigate and discipline public company auditors. The website contains all the latest information on standard setting and quality review. The site also includes news/current events and links to a technical forum and a management forum."

Cramer once again stopped to place a sheet on the Elmo projector. The following information was displayed. "I'm handing you out a copy of this."

ACCOUNTING AND AUDITING WEBSITES

Financial Accounting:

Financial Accounting Standards Board	www.fasb.org
Governmental Accounting Standards Board	www.gasb.org
Federal Accounting Standards Advisory Board	www.fasab.gov
Securities Exchange Commission	www.sec.gov

Auditing:

GAO Governmental Auditing Standards (the Yellow Book)	www.gao.gov/govaud/ybk01.htm

Sarbanes-Oxley Act	www.sarbanes-oxley.com
Public Company Accounting Oversight Board	www.pcaob.com
Office of Management and Budget (OMB)	www.whitehouse.gov/omb/

International Accounting and Auditing:

International Accounting Standards Board (IASB)	www.iasb.org
Internal Federation of Accountants (IFAC)	www.ifac.org

An accounting practitioner must remain up-to-date regarding authoritative developments, as well as other issues and developments affecting the business environment. These reference sources are extremely useful in this process. You may use these sources as you develop your term paper on auditing the production accounting department of a petroleum company."

A student interrupted. "Professor Cramer, let's get real! Can anyone possibly keep up with all this material? Are accountants supposed to be like Superman or something?" The question resulted in considerable laughter from the class.

"No one expects us to have all this information memorized, but we have to know how to find the pertinent information when we face a problem. The business community, not to mention the government, expects a professional level of service from an accounting professional. To maintain confidence in the profession, it is essential that accountants, particularly those in public practice, understand and effectively utilize research. Certainly with the Internet, research is much quicker today than years ago."

Cramer looked at his Cartier watch. The time was close to the end of the class period. Consequently, he knew there would be no responses, but he asked anyway, "Does anyone have any further questions before we dismiss?"

As the students began closing their books and preparing to leave, Cramer said, "Okay, I'll see you next time." With that remark, the students quickly filed out of the room. Cramer, left alone and weary from his lecture, hurried to his office. In less than an hour he had to leave for the airport to pick up Slam. Slam would be surprised and disappointed at what the Coke audit had uncovered.

Cramer kept his professor's hat on and went back to his office to continue to work on an examination. He re-read question number ten.

10. The AICPA formally requires one of these two major audit procedures as a result of the *McKesson & Robbins* fraud decision:

    a.   Physical counting of cash and physical examination of inventory.
    b.   Physical examination of inventory and confirmation of receivables.
    c.   Reconciliation of cash and confirmation of receivables.
    d.   Confirmation of receivables and adequate evaluation of the footnotes.
    e.   None of the above.

He marked the correct answer "b" on the key scantron. In 1938, fictitious inventories and accounts receivable amounted to 20 percent of their assets or nearly $250 million. Phillip Musica recruited three brothers, operating under assumed names, to generate bogus sales documentation and to pay commissions to a shell distribution company.

Cramer then wrote the following question:

11. What statement is *false* with respect to statements in SAS No. 99?

    a.   Auditors do not make legal determination of whether fraud has occurred.
    b.   Unlike errors, fraud is intentional and usually involves deliberate concealment of the facts.
    c.   A properly planned and performed audit will detect a material misstatement resulting from fraud.
    d.   Professional skepticism is an attitude that includes a questioning mind and a critical assessment of audit evidence.
    e.   None of the above.

The correct answer was, of course, "c" again. As he told his students, "Finding fraud is difficult. It's like trying to load a bunch of frogs onto a wheelbarrow."

Cramer prepared a few more questions, and then he left for the airport.

Chapter 16

He preferred the precision of a balanced ledger, its promise of fiscal transparency, its devotion to a world defined by generally accepted accounting principles, to the wild, terminal justice of the hollow-tipped bullet.

—Christopher Reich

Once the alarm system was compromised, a thin figure took off a ski mask, gloves, and a heavy coat. He put the gloves back on as he walked toward a Coca-Cola machine. Only after drinking a Classic Coke and eating some peanut butter crackers did the silent figure go to work.

Taking a crowbar the dark intruder broke into a treasure room and moved to the nearest glass-enclosed case. He placed a large flashlight face down on the glass and turned it on. Next a large suction cup was placed on top of the glass, and a round circle was cut with a glass cutter in the glass. After placing the round glass on the floor, his gloved hands placed the jewelry and other precious items into a brown cloth sack. Methodically the prowler emptied nineteen other glass-enclosed cases. When a sack was full, he took the full sack and placed it into the secret compartment.

After the remaining eleven storage cases were emptied, the thief broke into another storage room. The diamonds on the Diamond Robe sparkled as the light of his flashlight hit them. It disappeared into a cloth sack. Two other gem-encrusted gowns were placed on top of the Diamond Robe. Like Santa Claus on the night before Christmas, the robber placed the heavy sack over his shoulder and carried it back to a second secret compartment. This second hid-ing place was almost full, so the thin prowler became more selective on his return to the storage room.

He decided against taking the reliquary of St. Paul the Hermit — no gems on it. But his small hands gently placed the reliquary of the Holy Cross into his cloth sack. He liked the very large blue stone on it. He softly counted the number of precious stones on a crosier showing the Holy Trinity. There were 22 rubies and two large sapphires. Another chalice had 10 rubies, 6 emeralds, and at least 4 unknown white stones.

A statue of an angel was too heavy; so also was a tray with a garden scene.

Forget about a 17th century goblet, a tray for ampullae, a plate with a scene of the annunciation, and two candlesticks. But he took one of two vases — he liked the eight big green stones — and one of three flint muskets. The last item placed into his sack was a monstrance with a golden crown on top. After dragging the sack back to the secret compartment, he found that the sack would not fit. He pulled out the monstrance, closed the door, and wrapped the monstrance in another sack. He placed the sack next to the Coca-Cola machine, and began drinking a Cherry Coke.

He had not found the Ruby gown. "It must be on the Black Madonna," he thought. He walked to the storage area, and put a rosary and a golden chain into his pockets. Then he walked into the library, and shined his flashlight onto the white polychrome ceiling painting. He rested in a large armchair with the coat-of-arms of the Paulite Order. "Not comfortable," he said softly.

Retracing his steps, he began picking up his equipment: suction cup, glass cutter, ski mask, and the heavy coat. "Wait a minute." He put everything down, and walked over and retrieved the two Coke crates. After placing them next to the drink machine, he put on his coat, and stuffed the ski mask into his right coat pocket. He picked up the sack with the monstrance, walked over to the window next to the door, and cut a round hole in it. He then opened the window, climbed out, shut the window, and placed the round piece of glass on the ground. Cautiously he made his way through the Lubomirski Gate, across the courtyard, and disappeared into the still morning darkness. In seventy more minutes the sun would shine on the Shrine of the Black Madonna.

* * *

Not until the second day after the burglary did it become public. A spokesperson for the Polish Catholic church indicated that there had been a significant robbery at the Jasna Gora Monastery. A reward of two million zoltys was offered for the recovery of the stolen sacred artifacts. The spokesperson assured the world that the priceless Black Madonna was safe.

An official of the Polish Communist party stated that the robbery probably had been planned by a few Solidarity members to help improve Poland's economic situation. A Russian Kremlin official indicated that many Catholics suspected the "irresponsible hand of the CIA" in the "breaching of the security system" at the holy shrine. The State Department denied any knowledge of the unfortunate theft and offered any U.S. aid in recovering the stolen religious treasures.

A spokesman for the President said that the desperados would be found and punished. Many of the underground newspapers began carrying the following account of the robbery. "The bandits might have had inside help because the alarm system was off during the entry into the monastery. The only other logical conclusion is that someone forgot to switch on the silent alarm system (a highly coincidental accident). Or else the alarm system was faulty, which an official of the Paulite Order denied."

Another newspaper indicated that the Diamond robe, two other gowns, and the priceless "Aaron and Melchizedek" monstrance were part of the stolen artifacts. The robbers apparently made no attempt to take the Black Madonna, who fortunately was wearing the Ruby robe.

Chapter 17

Following the high incidence of defective and error prone systems, data and asset mishandling, and fraud, there is a great need for all concerned to learn how to secure, control, and audit computerized systems by prescribing effective controls to prevent, detect, and correct errors, minimize system improprieties, and protect data.

—Michael J. Cerullo

This week Laura was participating in a Finnish seminar dealing with "Russia as a Business Partner." The first three days of the seminar had taken place in Helsinki, Finland. The Finnish Export Institute suggests that Helsinki is the gateway to Russia. Located in the northernmost corner of Europe between Sweden and Russia, Finland is the home of Santa Claus, saunas, and reindeer meat. Laura was told that much business was transacted in saunas, but she did not ask if there were many female business executives in Finland.

So far the seminar was interesting, covering Russia's economic system and practical advice for conducting business in Russia. The Russian government was pushing joint ventures with foreign partners. A joint venture is not part of the planned system, so it functions as an absolutely independent production unit answerable for all its operations exclusively with its own resources.

Another way of dealing with Russian companies is through a buyback agreement. Since rubles are worthless outside of Russia, the major problem is how to get profits out of the country. For example, for many years Pepsi-Cola Company took its profits out in the form of vodka. Since Russia prefers to trade goods for goods because of their deficit of foreign currency, Pepsi signed a deal to trade

Pepsi-Colas, pizzas, and Kentucky Fried Chicken for petroleum worth nearly $2.6 billion.

Laura had been slightly shocked when she arrived at the best hotel in Moscow, the Mezhdunarodnaja, from the Moscow airport. The modern hotel looked like a Hyatt Regency, with a large open inside area with five glass elevators serving thirteen floors. Inside the lobby was a bright red Coke machine—Ko-Ka Kora. Of course, it took her about 20 minutes to purchase a token for two dollars to obtain a real Coke.

There was a round American Express money machine and advertising inside the large, open lobby. There was a large sign for the Chamber of Commerce, United Airlines, Wesotra (a transportation association), and BNL (an Italian Bank). The shops in the hotel took only hard currency and not Russian rubles.

Laura walked on the white tile floor to look at one of the many birch trees inside the lobby. The trunk of the tree was real, but the branches and leaves were fake. There were bright maroon carpets, chairs, and round tables around a water fountain with several large pools containing large red fish. There was a large, wooden-like clock seven stories high with a rooster on top. While Laura was checking into the hotel, the rooster began to crow on the hour, flapped its wings, and two wooden men began blowing their horns. What a sight.

Jet lag caused Laura to awake at 5:30 on Friday morning, so she decided to write Slam rather than e-mailing him. She knew the letter would arrive later than her flight back on Saturday evening, but she wanted to determine how long an express mail letter would take from Russia.

> Dear Great One,
>   I'm looking out of the 12th floor from the best hotel in Moscow. I can see a large river, smoke stacks, and red brick buildings. It's early in the morning, so there isn't much traffic on the roads yet.
>   All is fine. The conference is a success. I saw Red Square and the Cathedral of St. Basil yesterday. Also went to Gum Department Store.

The sky seems to be constantly smoggy here. I have yet
to really see the sun.

I look forward to seeing you when I return to the
States on Saturday. Europe isn't as fun without you.

Love Laura

After the seminar, Laura went with the group of eighteen Americans to the famous round Bolshoi Theatre to see a Polish ballet.
The stately and brightly decorated interior had six rows of red vel-
vet upholstery and gilded boxes with sparkling cut glass chandeliers. The frieze in front had red flags and two images of Lenin.
There were many figures of people on the round ceiling.

The ballet was shocking by Moscow atheist standards. It was a
bizarre, avant-garde ballet with many symbols. There was Christ
ascending into heaven, Mary at a tombstone, and flying nuns.
Laura first thought that a very loud scene was a UFO landing, but
it was instead the bombing of Poland in World War II. There was
little clapping from the audience, and a number of people left
early. One businessman joked that many of the Putin people left
early in disgust.

* * *

"What a boring movie and flight," thought Laura Lee Bertone
on her flight from New York to Atlanta. She was thinking about all
the fun she had missed during her fast-paced twenty-seven years.
She had been so busy with work, particularly in the computer area,
that she had had little time for romance — until Slam Duncan had
wandered into her life.

When the plane landed, she couldn't wait to get out of the "Big
Hustle" airport terminal. Atlanta's biggest employer is the airport.
This business trip had been hectic. She really wished Slam had not
been called back early. Slam would have made the return trip much
more enjoyable. She didn't realize how important Slam had become to her until he wasn't around, and she felt a lonesome ache
without him. She needed to do some soul searching and determine
if she should be more honest with Slam.

Laura considered herself very cultured. She liked good food, wine, nice clothes, and when she traveled she liked to go first class. She was independent, so where did Slam fit in? She was perplexed.

The plane taxied around the Hartsfield International Airport an insufferably long time after landing—even for Atlanta. Finally, the passengers were told they could disembark. As usual, several people had already stood up to get their carry-on bags, before the plane came to a complete stop at the terminal.

As she walked from the plane she spotted Slam in the crowd. She smiled at this pleasant surprise. "How sweet," she thought, "he's come to the airport to welcome me home."

Slam's gray eyes met hers. They were cold. He wasn't smiling. "What's wrong," she thought. Now they were only a few feet away from each other. Suddenly she noticed two Atlanta cops standing beside Slam.

"That's her," he said sadly.

Her heart was in her throat. She could not take a breath. Her mind raced with thoughts. "They can't know. Slam, Slam, what have you done?" She felt the policemen's hands grab her shoulders. She did not resist. One of the policemen told her rights. It seemed like a dream—no, a waking nightmare. A shudder came over her. As they escorted her to the police car, she looked over at Slam. He would not look at her. "Was that a look of anguish on his face?"

After driving her to the downtown police station, she was taken to an interrogation room. Slam came into the small room. The officers left and locked the door, leaving Slam and Laura alone.

"Don't you see?" he asked. "You're finished! We're finished!" He sat down hard in one of the wooden, straight-back chairs.

"Slam, I love you." She choked on the words.

"No matter," Slam said painfully. "While we were in Poland, Cramer cracked the case. He asked me to fly home early to prepare me for this wonderful reunion. He was afraid you might try to frame me and drag me down with you. I didn't believe him at first, but then he showed me evidence of what you've been doing."

He looked sternly into Laura's eyes.

"The night after we left on our trip, Cramer used the electronic spying equipment that I originally purchased to tap Loebbecke's computer. I thought Loebbecke was our Coke culprit. Cramer thought Loebbecke was too obvious. Turns out he was right. Cramer had a hunch that your computer knowledge would make it possible for you to pull off the Coke computer system shenanigans. But what really tipped him off was when he discovered you had worked with Loebbecke before he retired from Coke. You probably learned his computer password at that time and used it to throw us off your trail. You clandestinely entered the Coke computer system using a Trojan Horse program. I can't determine whether you wrote the program or simply discovered it. No matter. We got rid of it."

"To make a long story short, Cramer parked in front of your apartment and recorded images from your computer. When you used your laptop in Poland to dial into your computer back home in Atlanta, Cramer saw the Coke formula that you had derived from inventory records. You even made the mistake of using your computer to send messages over the Internet offering the formula for sale to people in India. Cramer has it all recorded."

"What! How?" Her face paled.

Slam ignored her question. "You knew that India tried to obtain the Coke formula many years ago. When Coke would not disclose the secret formula, India kicked Coke out of the country until the mid-nineties. India replaced Coke with a similar looking soft drink. Apparently, the cloned cola doesn't taste too good. You decided to sell the formula to your contacts in India for four million dollars. Not bad pay."

"Okay, so you know how I figured out the Coke formula. Is that illegal? You can't prove I tried to sell it. All you have is circumstantial evidence. Someone else may have been using my computer to send messages."

"Laura, it's over. Why don't you just give up? We also know you're the one who masterminded the theft of artifacts from the Jasna Gora religious site. While you were on your return plane trip, the Polish police arrested Martin Wojdak. He immediately confessed how you arranged for him to be the driver to service the Coke machines at Jasna Gora. Four months ago, working together, y'all had those specially reconstructed machines placed at the site. I overheard you ask him 'Are they in place?'"

Laura looked totally shattered, but said nothing.

Slam continued. "Cramer discovered that sales were down dramatically after the old drink machines were replaced. The declining sales stuck out like a sore thumb on the monthly sales reports. Why would sales decline due to new machines? After the Poland theft made the papers a few days ago, Cramer figured it might be related to those Coke machines. He called the Poles. They checked out the drink machines. Most of the religious artifacts were found in the two secret compartments in the backs of the machines. The police then apprehended Wojdak at home. He had already taken a few items to his house, and there was no way he could deny the theft. Naturally, he didn't try to protect you. In fact, he claims you blackmailed him to do it. He says you threatened to fire him if he didn't help you."

"He's lying. You can't prove anything!" Laura shouted.

"Laura! Shut up! We know everything! The police obtained a search warrant for your apartment. While looking for anything connected to the Poland robbery, they found some white powder hidden in a bag in the back of your closet. They were surprised when it was not identified as cocaine! I wasn't. The voodoo powder is now just one more item in the stack of evidence against you. Laura, you murdered an innocent student, and you nearly killed me!"

Laura tried to interrupt, but Slam continued.

"So far I haven't been able to break into all your computer files, but eventually I will. And when I do, I suspect I'll find a program that sends subliminal messages about flying."

"Slam, you must believe me," she pleaded. "The Zombie powder wasn't supposed to kill you, but just scare you off. I don't know why that student died. He must have had a bad reaction. And I don't know anything about subliminal messages!"

Slam stood up slowly and said, "I can't believe a word you say. I loved you once, but that's over."

Laura looked into Slam's eyes. When their eyes met, she thought his gaze would burn a hole through her. She had to turn away. She was more afraid than ever before in her life. She had lost everything.

With a shake of his head, Slam turned and walked quickly out of the room. He decided to go back to work on his dissertation. Writing about expert systems was certainly safer than auditing Coca-Cola.

The front-page bold headline in the Atlanta Constitution on Thursday proclaimed: "Black Madonna Trips Programmer's Scheme." A copyrighted story by Hugh Nations began as follows:

> Black Madonna was almost ripped off by Ms. Laura Lee Bertone, a computer whiz working for Coca-Cola. She attempted to steal valuable, religious artifacts from the Jasna Gora, the religious site of the Black Madonna. This high-achieving employee almost pulled it off with the help of two Coca-Cola machines with false-backs. A small individual hid in the Coke machine during the day, came out at night, and disarmed the security system.
>
> Aside from the millions to be earned from the theft of the artifacts, Laura Lee Bertone, almost sold the Coca-Cola formula to certain individuals from India for $4 million. Two alert forensic accountants stopped both schemes by checking accounting records prepared in Poland. Dr. Lenny Cramer, at Georgia State University and Mr. Beauregard (Slam) Duncan—

* * *

A computer's operating system keeps a directory, much like a telephone directory, of the name and location of each file. When a user deletes a file, the operating system does not remove the data. Instead, it indicates that the space is available; the contents remain in place until some other process overwrites them. The treatment of "deleted" files is comparable to a telephone company that deletes a subscriber from the phone book but leaves that customer's service active. Someone who knows the phone number can still call the subscriber in question. Similarly, someone who knows how to access these released-but-not-erased areas, and who has the proper tools, can recover their contents.

Johnette Hassell
Susan Steen

Panel 1

PCAOB: The Integrated Audit Process

Auditing Standard No. 5 indicates that the audit of internal control should be integrated with the audit of the financial statements. This means that the auditor should plan and perform the work to achieve the objectives of both audits,[1] which are as follows:

- *Audit of the financial statements.* To obtain reasonable assurance about whether the financial statements are presented fairly in accordance with GAAP.
- *Audit of internal control.* To obtain reasonable assurance about whether internal control over financial reporting is effective.

This appendix illustrates one approach for integrating the audit of internal control with the audit of the financial statements and is not intended to present all of the procedures that are required for a particular audit. Auditors should plan and perform their integrated audits to achieve the objectives of the audits and to comply with standards of the PCAOB.

Summary of the Illustrative Audit Approach

The integrated audit process can be summarized into the following major components:

    a.   Preliminary engagement procedures
    b.   Audit planning
    c.   Risk assessment procedures
    d.   Auditor response, including tests of accounts and controls
    e.   Conclusion and wrap-up

Preliminary Engagement Procedures

Preliminary engagement procedures include the auditor's engagement acceptance process and reaching an understanding with the audit committee about the terms of the engagement, including pre-approval of audit and non-audit services.

During the engagement acceptance process, the auditor might identify matters that could affect the risk of material misstatement of the financial statements or the risk of material weakness in internal control and thus could inform the auditor's risk assessments during the audit.

Audit Planning

During audit planning, the auditor should make a preliminary judgment about materiality. The judgment about materiality is the same for both the audit of the financial statements and the audit of internal control. The auditor also can develop a preliminary audit strategy and audit plan based on his or her understanding of the company and its environment. The audit strategy could cover matters such as general scope and timing of the engagement. The audit strategy and plan could be refined further as the audit progresses.

Risk Assessment Procedures

Risk assessment procedures are intended to help the auditor identify risks of misstatement and the controls that are in place to address those risks. When performing risk assessment procedures, the auditor should obtain an understanding of the company and its environment, including its internal control. These procedures include evaluating entity-level controls and walkthroughs, or other procedures to understand the likely sources of misstatement.[2] It also includes performing preliminary analytical procedures and procedures to assess the risk of material misstatement due to fraud. The auditor's risk identification and assessment should also take into account his or her knowledge about the company and its environment from other sources, such as prior audits.

Based on the auditor's understanding gained through performing the risk assessment procedures and obtaining other evidence, the auditor should assess the identified risks.

The auditor's risk assessments are the basis for the identification of significant accounts and disclosures and relevant assertions as well as the selection of controls to test. Relevant assertions and significant accounts and disclosures should be determined based on whether there is a reasonable possibility that they could contain misstatements that could cause the financial statements to be materially misstated.[3]

The identification of relevant assertions and significant accounts[4] is the same for both the audit of internal control and the audit of the financial statements.

Auditing Standard No. 5 states that the auditor should use a top-down approach to the audit of internal control to select the controls to test. A top-down approach begins at the financial statement level and with the auditor's understanding of the overall risks to internal control over financial reporting.[5] The auditor then focuses on entity-level controls and works down to significant accounts and disclosures and their relevant assertions. This approach directs the auditor's attention to accounts, disclosures, and assertions that present a reasonable possibility of material misstatement to the financial statements and related disclosures. The auditor then verifies his or her understanding of the risks in the company's processes and selects for testing those controls that sufficiently address the assessed risk of misstatement to each relevant assertion.

Overall Response to Risks

Based on the auditor's risk assessment, the auditor should evaluate the need for an overall response to the risks. This evaluation is particularly important for pervasive risks of misstatement, which can affect many financial statement accounts, but it applies to every audit.

The overall responses could affect such aspects of the audit as—

- Assignment of staff
- Level of supervision
- Need for specialists
- Level of professional skepticism
- Appropriateness of planned audit strategy and scope

Specific Responses — Substantive Procedures and Tests of Controls

Specific responses to risk relate to the tests of relevant assertions of significant accounts and disclosures ("substantive procedures") and the controls over those assertions. Auditing Standard No. 5 requires the auditor to obtain evidence about the controls over relevant assertions, and it states that the auditor should perform substantive procedures for all relevant assertions, regardless of the assessed level of control risk.[6] The auditor should determine an appropriate mix of the nature, timing, and extent of testing based on the associated risks and other factors.[7] The determination of the nature, timing and extent of testing includes decisions about using the work of others to test controls in the integrated audit. As the associated risk increases, the evidence that the auditor should obtain also increases. The relationship between tests of controls and substantive procedures is important to the integration of the audit of internal control with the audit of financial statements. Obtaining sufficient evidence to support control risk assessments as low for purposes of the financial statement audit ordinarily allows the auditor to reduce the amount of substantive procedures that otherwise would have been necessary to opine on the financial statements. On the other hand, deficiencies in the controls that the auditor planned to rely on could lead the auditor to expand his or her substantive procedures.

As discussed in Chapter 1, the results of substantive tests of accounts and disclosures do not provide sufficient evidence for the auditor to conclude on the operating effectiveness of controls. However, the results of substantive tests could affect the auditor's risk assessments associated with the controls. For example, if the results of substantive procedures indicate misstatements in an assertion, evaluating the nature, cause, and significance of the misstatements could lead the auditor to identify a deficiency in the related controls or modify his or her risk assessments. When no misstatements are detected from substantive procedures for an assertion, the auditor should take that into account along with the factors discussed in paragraphs 46–49 of Auditing Standard No. 5 in considering the risk associated with the related controls, which af-

fects the nature, timing, and extent of the testing necessary to conclude on the effectiveness of the controls.[8]

Conclusion and Wrap-Up

In the conclusion and wrap-up phase, the auditor should evaluate the results of his or her testing, particularly for identified misstatements and control deficiencies. The auditor should evaluate
the misstatements and control deficiencies, individually and in the
aggregate, based on quantitative and qualitative factors.

Based on the evaluation of the testing results, the auditor should
form conclusions about whether—

- The financial statements are materially misstated,
- A material weakness in internal control exists, and
- He or she has obtained sufficient competent evidence to sup-
  port those conclusions.

The results of each portion of the integrated audit inform the
auditor's conclusions about the other portion. For example, the
auditor's conclusions about the effectiveness of controls should be
based on all of the pertinent information about control effectiveness, including—

- Tests of controls for the audit of internal control,
- Tests of controls for the audit of the financial statements,
- Use of the work of others in either audit, and
- Evidence about control deficiencies resulting from identified
  misstatements or other sources (e.g., control deficiencies iden-
  tified by management).

This information could affect the conclusions about control effectiveness as of year-end as well as control risk assessments for the
financial statement audit. In some situations, the evaluation of audit
results also could lead the auditor to re-evaluate his or her assessments
of risk and the sufficiency of the audit procedures performed.

The conclusion and wrap-up phase of the audit also includes
completion of the review of the audit and resolution of reviewers'
comments.

Source: PCAOB, "Guidance for Auditors of Smaller Public Companies," October 17, 2007.

Notes

1. See Auditing Standard No. 5, paragraph 6.
2. See Auditing Standard No. 5, paragraphs 34–38, for discussion of the objectives of walkthroughs and direction on walkthrough procedures.
3. See Auditing Standard No. 5, paragraphs 28–33.
4. In the financial statement audit, the auditor may perform substantive auditing procedures on financial statement accounts, disclosures and assertions that are not determined to be significant accounts and disclosures and relevant assertions. This is because his or her assessment of the risk that undetected misstatement would cause the financial statements to be materially misstated is unacceptably high (see AU sec. 312.39 for further discussion about undetected misstatement) or as a means of introducing unpredictability in the procedures performed (see AU sec. 316.50 for further discussion about predictability of auditing procedures).
5. See Auditing Standard No. 5, paragraph 21.
6. See Auditing Standard No. 5, paragraph B7.
7. For example, in the audit of internal control, walkthroughs might provide sufficient evidence of operating effectiveness for some selected controls, depending on the risk associated with the control being tested, the specific procedures performed as part of the walkthrough, and the results of those procedures.
8. This does not mean that the auditor is required to perform substantive procedures for a relevant assertion before performing tests of controls.

Panel 2

COSO's Enterprise Risk Management

Eight components make up ERM framework:

1. *Internal Environment*—provides the framework for ERM and is comprised of an organization's ethical values, competence and development of personnel, and management's operating style and how it assigns authority and responsibility. The Board of Directors and management must work together in establishing the organization's risk philosophy (attitude toward risk), risk appetite (level of risk the organization can tolerate), and risk culture (attitudes towards risks encountered on a day-to-day basis).

2. *Objective Setting*—must be established by management, aligned to the organization's mission/vision, consistent with the organization's risk appetite, and measurable. Objectives can be either strategic, operational, reporting, or compliance.

3. *Event Identification*—considers happenings that could (positively or negatively) affect the organization's ability to meet its objectives. Management should consider the impact that various factors may have on the likelihood that particular events may occur. Internal factors include infrastructure, personnel, process, and technology. External factors include economic, business, natural environment, political, social, and technological factors.

4. *Risk Assessment*—allows the entity to consider the likelihood and impact that events will affect the achievement of objectives.

5. *Risk Response*—requires management to select a response that is expected to bring risk likelihood and impact within the entity's risk tolerance. Risk responses fall into the categories of risk avoidance, reduction, sharing, and acceptance. Risk avoidance involves discontinuing the related activity. Risk reduction involves implementing controls that reduce either the likelihood or impact of the event. Risk sharing occurs when other parties accept a portion of an event's risk. Finally, acceptance means that management is willing to accept the likelihood and impact of a particular event.

6. *Control Activities*—are the policies and procedures that help ensure risk responses are properly executed. General controls affect an entire organization, whereas application controls are designed to ensure completeness, accuracy, authorization, and validity of data capture and transaction processing.

7. *Information and Communication*—from internal and external sources must be identified, captured, and communicated in a form and timeframe that enable personnel to carry out their responsibilities. Information is a basis for communication, which must meet the expectations of groups and individuals to enable them to effectively carry out their responsibilities.

8. *Monitoring*—is a process that assesses both the presence and functioning of ERM and its components and the quality of its performance over time. Monitoring may occur through ongoing activities or as separate evaluations. The results of monitoring should be given to those responsible for ERM including upper management and the board of directors.

Panel 3

Some Infamous Recent Financial Statement Frauds

- Tyco
  - Large interest-free loans to officers; then forgiven ($87.1 million).
  - Unauthorized bonuses (no approval of BOD).
  - Fake documents showing no loans outstanding.
  - SEC found that PwC had prior knowledge of fraud back to 1998.
  - Undisclosed real estate transaction with related parties.
  - False entries in books to cover-up bribes given to foreign officials.

- Adelphia [Greek for brothers]
  - Moved debt to subsidiaries which were not consolidated.
  - Personal loans to the Rigas family (self-dealing).
  - Falsified operations statistics and inflated earnings.

- Xerox
  - Accelerated revenues from leasing equipment.
  - Cookie jar reserves.

- Sunbeam
  - Cookie-jar restructuring reserves.
  - Channel stuffing.
  - Guaranteed sales.
  - Improper bill and hold.

- Waste Management
  - Reduced depreciation expense by inflating salvage value and extending useful lives.
  - No write-offs for unsuccessful land projects.
  - Improperly capitalized a number of expenses.
  - Made top drawer adjustments.

- HPL Technologies (2001–2002)
  - Created many fake purchase orders from Canon sales (a Japanese distributor). Printed and pasted Canon signatures on the documents.
  - Altered bank records to create millions of dollars in nonexistence customer payments.
  - Borrowed millions from his brokerage account (secured by HPL stock) and channeled the funds into the company in the form of payments.

- Baptist Foundation of Arizona
  - Set up subsidiaries owned by insiders to buy real estate (which had crashed in value) from BFA.
  - BFA then recorded notes receivables in the amount of the book values.
  - Ran a Ponzi scheme using new investors' money to pay old investors high returns.
  - Refused to give Arthur Andersen financial statements of the subsidiaries.

Panel 4

Auditing Hints

- SAS No. 99 does not require auditors to make inquiries of "others," as opposed to management. Auditors must talk to and interview others below management level. If asked, employees may be willing to report suspicious activities.
- Use independent sources for evaluating management (e.g., financial analysts). Surf the Internet.
- Auditors need to follow the performance history of managers and directors.
- If a company has an anonymous reporting system, obtain information about the incidents reported and consider them when assessing fraud risk.
- Be sure to perform analytical procedures, and the work should be reviewed by senior members of the audit team.
- Auditors should select sample items below their normal testing scope (e.g., HealthSouth).
- Fraud procedures should be more than checklists. Audits should focus on finding and detecting fraud.
- Ask for and review all "top drawer" entries.
- Ask for and review all side agreements.

Panel 5

Abusive Earnings Management

- Improper revenue recognition (e.g., bill and hold sales).
- Improper expense recognition.
- Using reserves to inflate earnings in years with falling revenues (cookie jar accounting).
- Shifting debt to special purpose entities (SPEs).
- Channel stuffing.
- Capitalizing marketing costs rather than expensing.
- Extending useful lives and inflating salvage values.
- Accelerating revenue from leasing equipment.
- SPEs not consolidated.

Panel 6

Communications About Control Deficiencies in an Audit of Financial Statements — AU Section 325

1. In an audit of financial statements, the auditor may identify deficiencies in the company's internal control over financial reporting. A control deficiency exists when the design or operation of a control does not allow management or employees, in the normal course of performing their assigned functions, to prevent or detect misstatements on a timely basis.

- A deficiency in design exists when (a) a control necessary to meet the control objective is missing or (b) an existing control is not properly designed so that, even if the control operates as designed, the control objective would not be met.
- A deficiency in operation exists when a properly designed control does not operate as designed or when the person performing the control does not possess the necessary authority or qualifications to perform the control effectively.

2. A *significant deficiency* is a deficiency, or a combination of deficiencies, in internal control over financial reporting, that is less severe than a material weakness yet important enough to merit attention by those responsible for oversight of the company's financial reporting.

3. A *material weakness* is a deficiency, or a combination of deficiencies, in internal control over financial reporting, such that there is a reasonable possibility that a material misstatement of the

company's annual or interim financial statements will not be prevented or detected on a timely basis.

Note: There is a reasonable possibility of an event when the likelihood of the event is either "reasonably possible" or "probable," as those terms are used in paragraph 3 of Financial Accounting Standards Board Statement No. 5, *Accounting for Contingencies*.

Note: In evaluating whether a deficiency exists and whether deficiencies, either individually or in combination with other deficiencies, are material weaknesses, the auditor should follow the direction in paragraphs 62-70 of PCAOB Auditing Standard No. 5, *An Audit of Internal Control Over Financial Reporting That Is Integrated with An Audit of Financial Statements*.

4. The auditor must communicate in writing to management and the audit committee all significant deficiencies and material weaknesses identified during the audit. The written communication should be made prior to the issuance of the auditor's report on the financial statements. The auditor's communication should distinguish clearly between those matters considered significant deficiencies and those considered material weaknesses, as defined in paragraphs 2 and 3.

Note: If no such committee exists with respect to the company, all references to the audit committee in this standard apply to the entire board of directors of the company.

5. If oversight of the company's external financial reporting and internal control over financial reporting by the company's audit committee is ineffective, that circumstance should be regarded as an indicator that a material weakness in internal control over financial reporting exists. Although there is not an explicit requirement to evaluate the effectiveness of the audit committee's oversight in an audit of only the financial statements, if the auditor becomes aware that the oversight of the company's external financial reporting and internal control over financial reporting by the company's audit committee is ineffective, the auditor must communicate that information in writing to the board of directors.

Panel 7

Fraud Risk Assessment

To protect itself and its stakeholders effectively and efficiently from fraud, an organization should understand fraud risk and the specific risks that directly or indirectly apply to the organization. A structured fraud risk assessment, tailored to the organization's size, complexity, industry, and goals, should be performed and updated periodically. The assessment may be integrated with an overall organizational risk assessment or performed as a stand-alone exercise, but should, at a minimum, include risk identification, risk likelihood and significance assessment, and risk response.

Fraud risk identification may include gathering external information from regulatory bodies (e.g., securities commissions), industry sources (e.g., law societies), key guidance setting groups (e.g., Cadbury,[1] King Report, and The Committee of Sponsoring Organizations of the Treadway Commission (COSO)), and professional organizations (e.g., The Institute of Internal Auditors (IIA), the American Institute of Chartered Accountants (CICA), The CICA Alliance for Excellence in Investigative and Forensic Accounting, The Association of Certified Chartered Accountants (ACCA), and the International Federation of Accountants (IFAC), plus others noted in Appendix A of this document). Internal sources for identifying fraud risks should include interviews and brainstorming with personal representing a broad spectrum of activities within the organization, review of whistleblower complaints, and analytical procedures.

---

1. The Cadbury Report refers to The Report of the Committee on the Financial Aspects of Corporate Governance, issued by the United Kingdom on Dec. 10, 1992 and the King Report refers to the King Report on Corporate Governance for South Africa, issued in 1994.

An effective fraud risk identification process includes an assessment of the incentives, pressures, and opportunities to commit fraud. Employee incentive programs and the metrics on which they are based can provide a map to where fraud is most likely to occur. Fraud risk assessment should consider the potential override of controls by management as well as areas where controls are weak or there is a lack of segregation of duties.

The speed, functionality, and accessibility that created the enormous benefits of the information age have also increased an organization's exposure to fraud. Therefore, any fraud risk assessment should consider access and override of system controls as well as internal and external threats to data integrity, system security, and theft of financial and sensitive business information.

Assessing the likelihood and significance of each potential fraud risk is a subjective process that should consider not only monetary significance, but also significance to an organization's financial reporting, operations, and reputation, as well as legal and regulatory compliance requirements. An initial assessment of fraud risk should consider the inherent risk[2] of a particular fraud in the absence of any known controls that may address the risk.

Individual organizations will have different risk tolerances. Fraud risks can be addressed by establishing practices and controls to mitigate the risk, accepting the risk—but monitoring actual exposure—or designing ongoing or specific fraud evaluation procedures to deal with individual fraud risks. An organization should strive for a structured approach versus a haphazard approach. The benefits an implemented fraud risk management program provides should not exceed its cost. Management and board members should ensure the organization has the appropriate control mix in place, recognizing their oversight duties and responsibilities in terms of the organization's sustainability and their role as fiduciaries to stakeholders, depending on organizational form. Management is re-

---

2. Interent risk is the risk before considering any internal controls in place to mitigate such risk.

Source: Managing The Business Risk of Fraud, IIA, AICPA, ACFE, 2008, pp. 7–8.

sponsible for developing and executing mitigating controls to address fraud risks while ensuring controls are executed efficiently by competent and objective individuals.

Panel 8

Other Books by Larry Crumbley

- *The Big R: A Forensic Accounting Action Adventure*, Carolina Academic Press, 919-489-7486; Fax 919-493-5668. $25.00
- *Deadly Art Puzzle: Accounting for Murder* (advanced accounting), Thomson Corp., 800-355-9983; Fax 800-487-8488; In Europe, Tel: 44-207-0672500 (UK). $21.95
- *Simon the Incredible* (finance), Thomson Corp., 800-355-9983; Fax 800-487-8488; In Europe, Tel: 44-207-0672500 (UK). $24.95
- *The Bottom Line is Betrayal* (general business), Thomson Corp., 800-355-9983; Fax 800-487-8488; In Europe, Tel: 44-207-0672500 (UK). $23.95
- *Costly Reflections in a Midas Mirror* (cost/managerial accounting), Thomas Horton & Daughters, PO Box 23, Glen Ridge, NJ 07028, 973-566-9998, Fax: 973-429-1893. $9.95
- *Accosting the Golden Spire* (basic accounting), Thomas Horton & Daughters, PO Box 23, Glen Ridge, NJ 07028, 973-566-9998, Fax: 973-429-1893. $9.95
- *The Ultimate Rip-off: A Taxing Tale* (taxation), Thomas Horton & Daughters, PO Box 23, Glen Ridge, NJ 07028, 973-566-9998, Fax: 973-429-1893. $9.95
- *Computer Encryptions in Whispering Caves* (accounting information systems), Dame Publishing Company, 1998, $24.95
- *Chemistry in Whispering Caves* (chemistry), Thomson Corp., 800-355-9983; Fax 800-487-8488; In Europe, Tel: 44-207-0672500 (UK), 1998, $24.95

- *Nonprofit Sleuths: Follow the Money* (governmental accounting), Thomson Corp., 800-355-9983; Fax 800-487-8488; In Europe, Tel: 44-207-0672500 (UK), 1997, $24.95
- Greenspan, *Burmese Caper* (finance), Thomas Horton & Daughters, PO Box 23, Glen Ridge, NJ 07028, 973-566-9998, Fax: 973-429-1893. 1991, $9.95